Allergy-Free
Cooking for Kids

A guide to childhood
food intolerance with 80 recipes

Antoinette Savill
with Karen Sullivan

 thorsons

For my father who loved good food
and Grandma who loved baking

Thorsons
An Imprint of HarperCollins*Publishers*
77–85 Fulham Palace Road,
Hammersmith, London W6 8JB

The website address is: www.thorsonselement.com

and *Thorsons* are trademarks of
HarperCollins*Publishers* Ltd

First published by Thorsons in 2003

1 3 5 7 9 10 8 6 4 2

© Antoinette Savill and Karen Sullivan 2003

Antoinette Savill and Karen Sullivan assert the moral right
to be identified as the authors of this work

A catalogue record of this book
is available from the British Library

ISBN 0 00 714216 1

Photographs © Dave King

Printed and bound in Great Britain by
Scotprint, Haddington, East Lothian

Contents

Introduction

Food has the ability to heal and nourish. A healthy diet can make us feel uplifted and bursting with energy, and creates a foundation for good health on all levels. But for some people, food becomes a minefield. It can represent a threat not only to physical and emotional health, but even to life. The natural, essential act of eating becomes fraught with problems, with the result that something that should be pleasurable and life enhancing becomes tiresome, worrying and ultimately the object of fear.

As adults, we can monitor what we eat and analyse foods that make us feel well or ill; we can take precautions to ensure we avoid foods that can be problematic – by reading labels, cooking and purchasing food sensibly, and adapting our lifestyles to fit around allergies that can threaten our health. Children, however, are a different story. We have a natural instinct to nurture and protect our children, and a great responsibility to ensure their health, both now and in the future. What our children eat will define their daily existence and prepare them for a healthy future. When they suffer from allergies that endanger their lives, or even simply cause the type of niggling health problems that affect their growth, development and day-to-day living, we can feel inadequate, fearful and rightly concerned that they will be unable to live normal lives and become healthy, happy adults.

Children can be taught to understand their health problems, but the chances are they will feel isolated and 'different' when their diets are unlike those of their friends and the daily fare and treats that punctuate the average child's life simply do not exist. It is a huge challenge for parents of allergic and food-intolerant or food-sensitive children to ensure that their children's diets are both balanced and nutritious, as well as being appealing, tempting, delicious and child-friendly. No child wants to be different and there is nothing worse than feeling like a social leper or an oddity at the age of six, let's say, or twelve.

All parents struggle to some degree to ensure that their children eat well. The junk food culture is overwhelmingly widespread and unnutritious kiddy food is undoubtedly the staple diet of far too many children. Coupled with the information and misinformation that abounds regarding food sensitivities and allergies, it is not surprising that many parents choose simply to give up and produce the same bland and unappealing 'safe' meals on a daily basis.

But children need variety to attain good health – they need a multitude of different nutrients to ensure that they grow and develop properly. What's more, they need to learn an enjoyment of good food and recognize that it does not need to pose a threat to their lives or their lifestyles. They need to have treats, as well as nourishing meals that engender healthy eating habits that will remain with them for the rest of their lives. They also need the basic elements of nutrition to ensure that they are strong and healthy enough to overcome allergies and sensitivities.

This book offers a mouthwatering selection of easy-to-prepare recipes designed especially for children's likes, palates, interests and needs. Before embarking on the recipes, however, it is important to understand the issues that surround food and children. Let's start by looking at the concept of food allergies and the theories that lie behind them. You may find this section surprisingly reassuring. Countless children – and an ever-increasing number – suffer from allergies and intolerance and it may not be as difficult as you think to arrange your child's diet to suit his or her needs.

Even parents of children without allergies have difficulty making sense of the plethora of issues that surround food, so we'll also look at what children really need and how you can ensure that an allergic child is getting the nuts and bolts of good nutrition.

The allergy equation

Food allergies are undoubtedly over-diagnosed and little understood and you may find that your child has a temporary condition rather than something deep-seated and long-lasting. A true food allergy is a serious issue and although food allergies are becoming increasingly common, so too are intolerances and sensitivities to foods. We'll look at the reasons behind the increases a little later; first, let's look at each type of reaction in detail.

Food allergies

Although they are becoming more common, true food allergies are not as prevalent as you might think. Less than one per cent of the population suffers from a true food allergy, although, for that one per cent, the reality of the situation can be extremely frightening. It is important to distinguish a food allergy from more common problems such as food intolerance, indigestion or other conditions.

Food allergies are quite different from intolerance and involve different parts of the body. A food allergy occurs when the immune system mistakenly believes that a harmless substance, in this case a particular food, is harmful. In its attempt to protect the body, it creates specific antibodies to that food. The next time you eat that food, the immune system releases high levels of chemicals and histamines in order to protect the body. These chemicals trigger a rush of allergic symptoms that can affect the respiratory system, gastrointestinal tract, skin or cardiovascular system.

Symptoms vary dramatically between sufferers, but they range from a tingling sensation in the mouth, swelling of the tongue and the throat, difficulty breathing, hives, vomiting, abdominal cramps and diarrhoea, to a drop in blood pressure, loss of consciousness and even death. Symptoms typically appear within minutes to two hours after the sufferer has eaten the food to which they are allergic. In most cases, symptoms set in quickly and dramatically. There may be an instant rash or hives on the skin, breathing may become laboured and there may be intense pain or full-blown diarrhoea within a short space of time.

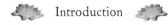

What causes food allergies?

The exact cause of food allergies is unknown, but there appears to be a genetic link. Children have a 40–70 per cent chance of developing allergies if both parents have allergies, depending on whether the parents share the same allergy. The risk drops to about 20–30 per cent with one allergic parent and to 10 per cent if the parents have no allergies. So if both you and your child's other parent suffer from a similar allergy, there is a strong chance that your child will as well. You can take steps to prevent this (see page 16), but avoiding problematic foods is a good idea until an allergy test can be arranged.

Because the immune system responds in an abnormal way to foods, it is possible that food allergies can be triggered by illness or even immunisation, as both leave the immune system in a weakened state and therefore more susceptible to allergens. In fact, you may have found that your child's symptoms first presented themselves following an illness or one of the scheduled injections.

About 70 per cent of food allergies develop in people younger than 30. As the body ages, the digestive system matures and the body is less likely to absorb food or food components that trigger allergies. Although it is possible to have food allergies at any age, children are 10 times more likely to have a food allergy than adults. Fortunately, children typically outgrow allergies to milk, wheat and eggs by about age six. Severe allergies and allergies to nuts and shellfish are more likely to be lifelong. Individuals of all ages are likely to lose sensitivities to milk, eggs and soya products more quickly than to fish, shellfish, peanuts and walnuts.

Another possible factor in food allergies, and certainly intolerance and sensitivities, is something called 'leaky gut syndrome'. Leaky gut syndrome is the name given to a common health disorder in which the intestinal lining is more permeable (porous) than normal. The abnormally large spaces present between the cells of the gut wall allow the entry of toxic material – bacteria, fungi, parasites, undigested protein, fat and waste – into the bloodstream that would, in healthier circumstances, be repelled and eliminated. This basically means that larger than usual protein molecules are being absorbed before they have a chance to be completely broken down. The immune system sees these molecules as foreign, invading substances and reacts by making antibodies against them in an attempt to destroy them.

The syndrome is caused by the inflammation of the gut lining, which can be brought about by the following:

- antibiotics – as these lead to the overgrowth of abnormal flora in the gastrointestinal tract (bacteria, parasites, candida, fungi)
- caffeine and many soft drinks, which are strong gut irritants and can be particularly dangerous for younger children
- chemicals in fermented and processed food (dyes, preservatives, peroxidised fats)
- enzyme deficiencies (e.g. coeliac disease, lactase deficiency causing lactose intolerance)
- NSAIDS (non-steroidal anti-inflammatory drugs, such as ibuprofen)

- prescription corticosteroids (e.g. prednisone)
- a highly refined carbohydrate diet (including chocolate bars, sweets, cakes, cookies, soft drinks and white bread)

All of these elements may, therefore, be implicated in food allergies, so it is worth taking a look at your child's diet as the foundation for the problems he or she is experiencing.

About 90 per cent of food allergies are triggered by certain proteins in:

COW'S MILK

EGG WHITES

PEANUTS

WHEAT

SOYA BEANS

Other common allergens include:

FISH

SHELLFISH

TREE NUTS

BEANS

CORN

STRAWBERRIES

TOMATOES

Can food allergies be cured?

The only way to avoid a reaction is to avoid allergy-causing foods completely. One of the most important things that you, as a parent, must do is to learn to read labels. Many products contain traces of foods that create a reaction, and must, by law, be noted on the label. However, you may find some labels feature unfamiliar terms – in which case either avoid the food completely or contact the manufacturer to ask for an explanation.

Processed foods are most likely to contain allergens, so it makes sense to avoid these wherever possible. While labelling has improved, there are always cases where warnings are not registered and this can create a serious and dangerous situation for a severe sufferer. Always go for fresh, whole foods. Not only are these healthier and much less likely to cause problems, but they will improve health, which is one of the keys to overcoming allergies. Many parents find it difficult to entertain the idea of relying entirely on home-cooked meals, with busy lifestyles and finicky children to contend with. The recipes in this book will make that job a lot easier.

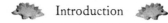

As I've already said, most people do outgrow their food allergies, although allergies to peanuts, nuts, shellfish and fish are often considered to be life-long. According to Dr Robert S. Zeiger, author of a study run by the Kaiser Permanente Medical Center in San Diego, the most common food allergies – to milk and eggs – tend to disappear by age three to five. However, in contrast to conventional wisdom, Dr Zeiger's study found that allergies to peanut and fish *can* pass by the age of seven – an age that seems to be a turning point in the development of the immune system.

The best way to address food allergies is to work on improving overall health, through diet and lifestyle. Because of the link between the gut and food allergies, it is also worth taking steps to heal the intestinal tract. It is also important to boost your child's immune system, so that he or she can deal more effectively both with allergens and with ordinary viruses and bacteria that can leave the body more susceptible to ill-health and further immune dysfunction.

Is your child's health at risk?

Over the past 10 to 15 years, research has begun to link many different childhood problems to food sensitivities. For example, colic, eczema, asthma, chronic catarrh, glue ear, headaches, migraine and even behavioural problems have all been traced back to certain foods or food additives. There is also evidence that children who show food sensitivity in their early years are more likely to develop other health problems later, often continuing into their adult lives. To ensure good long-term health, it is therefore crucial that any sensitivities are pin-pointed and dealt with early on.

Identifying food allergies

You may be confused by the issue of allergy testing, which appears to be the subject of some controversy. For example, *Which?* magazine in the UK found allergy tests to be unreliable and, they decided, a waste of money. Other experts don't agree. All severe allergies will be picked up by one of two tests (see below). What can be difficult to assess are food intolerances, the symptoms of which often show up hours or even days after the test. In addition, the symptoms of intolerance are often of an innocuous nature – for instance, bloating or headaches – and can easily be misread or mistaken for something else.

There are two main types of tests:

- The skin prick test is normally done in a doctor's or consultant's office, and involves placing a drop of the substance being tested on the patient's forearm or back and pricking the skin with a needle, allowing a tiny amount to enter the skin. If the patient is allergic to the substance, a wheal (mosquito bite-like bump) will form at the site within about 15 minutes.
- The radioallergosorbent test, or RAST, requires a blood sample. The sample is sent to a medical laboratory where tests are done with specific foods to determine whether the patient has antibodies to that food. This test is often used on young children who might become distressed by frequent skin 'pricks' and on children who have eczema or another skin condition that might make the results of a skin prick test difficult to assess.

If your child has experienced a dramatic reaction to a particular food in the past, don't rule out testing because you feel you have identified the culprit. Your child may have a serious allergy, but equally it may have been a one-off occurrence, when your child was rundown, for example, or it may have been something that he or she has already outgrown. Before taking steps to completely eliminate foods, it is sensible to ensure that you are actually dealing with a true food allergy and not something less sinister. It is worth noting, however, that neither of the above-mentioned tests is 100 per cent accurate. A negative test is more useful than a positive result; in these circumstances, it is highly unlikely that food is at the root of any health problems. Positive tests seem to be less reliable; in fact, some studies indicate that there may be as little as a 30 per cent chance that a true food allergy exists. You may need to undertake, with the help of your doctor, an elimination programme and keep a food diary (see page 14), to pinpoint the problem foods yourself.

Avoid cytotoxic testing and symptom provocation/neutralization testing, in which a dose of food extract is placed under the tongue. These tests are now known to be unreliable in detecting food allergies.

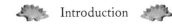

False food allergy

Confusing as it may sound, some foods, such as eggs, strawberries and shellfish, do not depend on antibodies being formed but instead trigger mast cells directly. Mast cells are basically special cells that are imbedded in the tissues in areas of the body (the lungs, the nose and the gut) vulnerable to invasion by parasites etc. The mast cells release so-called mediators, which are designed to fight off the invasion, and it is these that cause symptoms. The symptoms caused by mast cells releasing mediators are indistinguishable from true food allergies and obviously can be just as dangerous. Other foods known to cause this type of allergy are peanuts, legumes, fish, tomatoes, alcohol, chocolate and pork.

Distinguishing between a false and a true allergy isn't entirely crucial, as the consequences and the treatment are much the same. However, it appears that children with false food allergy may have some underlying deficiency that makes them more susceptible. For example, one study showed that 50 per cent of patients with false food allergy are deficient in magnesium. It is also more likely that children will grow out of a false food allergy, normally by the age of about eight, although the reasons for this are unknown.

Emergency treatment

Anaphylaxis is a sudden, severe, potentially fatal, systemic allergic reaction that can involve various areas of the body (such as the skin, respiratory tract, gastrointestinal tract and cardiovascular system). Symptoms occur within minutes to two hours after contact with the allergy-causing substance, but in rare instances may occur up to four hours later. Anaphylactic reactions can be mild to life-threatening. Children with asthma, eczema, or hay fever are at greater relative risk of experiencing anaphylaxis.

If your child suffers a severe reaction to a food (anaphylaxis), they may need an emergency injection of adrenaline (epinephrine) and many parents of serious allergy sufferers are provided with an 'epi-pen' to administer a shot if symptoms occur. In any case of anaphylaxis, it is recommended that you take your child to the emergency department of the nearest hospital.

If a reaction to certain foods is an annoyance but not life-threatening, your doctor may prescribe antihistamines to prevent the release of histamine by the immune system. Creams and lotions, such as calamine, hydrocortisone, and urtica are also used to ease symptoms that affect the skin.

Coping with an allergic child

- Education is the key. Your child will need to understand his or her condition and know how important it is to avoid problem foods. You don't need to be a scaremonger, but you do need to present the risks in such a way that they understand the potential severity. Try not to make your child feel 'different'. Simply point out to your child that he has special requirements and show him how to be diligent.
- Younger children will obviously not be able to make informed choices or decisions, so you will need to advise other parents, teachers and friends about the situation, and preplan. If your child is unable to eat the foods his friends are eating, find out in advance what is being served and see if you can produce something similar. The recipes in this book are all delicious and child-friendly, and allow you to create meals that are similar to those that your child's friends are eating.
- Be aware of common allergens and take care when introducing these foods (see page 18), particularly if there are allergies in your family.
- Send a supply of 'safe' snacks with your child to school and teach her not to swap. Educating children is the key to preventing attacks.
- Talk to your child's school about what foods are suitable and ensure that there is plenty of 'safe' food on the menu. If you are concerned, send a packed lunch. Above all, and once again, teach your child what she can and can't eat and explain what can happen if she is tempted to eat the wrong foods.
- Make your child's school aware of any allergies. Write a letter and highlight the specific foods in bold, or in a different coloured ink.
- Ask your child's teacher what projects (in art, or the science lab, for example) might contain foods that could cause a reaction. Find an alternative well in advance.
- Make sure your child and/or the school has access to emergency treatment (an epi-pen, for example) and that everyone involved learns how to recognize symptoms and knows how to administer treatment.
- Make sure your child has an allergy alert bracelet, or something on his person explaining his allergies. If he experiences an attack while away from people who are aware of the situation, this crucial information may save his life.

Food allergy facts

- According to the US Centers for Disease Control, in the US, 2–2½ per cent of the general population suffers from food allergy – that's 6–7 million Americans. Up to 3 million Americans suffer from peanut or tree nut (walnuts, pecans, etc.) allergy. It is estimated that in the US, as many as 125 people die each year from food allergy-related reactions.
- In the UK, as many as 1 in 200 people has a severe allergy to peanuts and at least 6 people die from it every year. Thousands more suffer from reactions to other foods, including milk, fish and eggs.
- Eight foods account for 90 per cent of allergic reactions. These are peanuts, tree nuts, fish, shellfish, eggs, milk, soya and wheat.
- Peanuts are the leading cause of severe allergic reactions, followed by shellfish, fish, tree nuts and eggs.
- Individuals with food allergies and asthma appear to be at an increased risk of severe allergic reaction.
- Most individuals who have had a reaction ate a food that they *thought* was safe.
- According to a study in the June 1995 issue of the *Journal of Allergy and Clinical Immunology,* high-risk infants who did not consume cow's milk, eggs and peanuts during infancy and whose mothers also avoided those foods during the perinatal period had a reduced incidence of food allergy and eczema in the first two years of life.
- In 1985, the *Lancet* reported that of 76 hyperactive children treated with a low-allergen diet, 62 improved and a normal range of behaviour was achieved in 21 of these. Other symptoms such as headaches and fits were often improved. Of the 48 foods incriminated, artificial colourings and preservatives were the most common provoking substances. The study reported that benzoic acid (preservative E210) and tartrazine (yellow food colouring E102) had a bad effect on nearly eight out of the ten children involved.

Food intolerance

Unlike food *allergy*, food *intolerance* does not involve the immune system. It is an adverse reaction caused by specific foods. For instance, lactose intolerance occurs when the sufferer lacks an enzyme that is needed to digest milk sugar (lactose). When that child (or adult) eats milk products, he or she will experience symptoms such as gas, bloating, diarrhoea and/or abdominal pain.

Interestingly, research shows that it is almost always the most commonly eaten foods that are the source of the problem. In Britain and in other Western countries, wheat and milk are key culprits, largely because they are consumed several times every day. In the US, sensitivity to corn (maize) is also very common, partly because it is present in so many prepared foods. Peanuts are another very common allergen in the US – possibly because peanut butter is so popular, but also because peanuts are a very common snack food.

In their book *The Complete Guide to Food Allergy and Intolerance*, the authors, Dr Jonathan Brostoff and Linda Gamlin, reported a remarkable link between the overconsumption of particular foods and subsequent sensitivities in patients, and claim that a large intake of any food, regardless of what it is, can trigger off intolerance of that food.

If you suspect an intolerance, it is important to look at the foods that make a regular appearance in your child's diet. It is easy to see how an intolerance can develop when you break down the average child's daily diet. Often their daily menu will run along the following lines: cereal and milk (or toast) for breakfast, a biscuit at break time, a sandwich (possibly cheese) for lunch, and pasta with tomato and cheese sauce for dinner. Every meal contains wheat and most contain dairy produce. This means that your child will, effectively, be eating the same foods constantly throughout the day, which can create sensitivities and compound intolerance. A little later, we'll look at ways to create a varied diet.

Causes of intolerance

While the immune system is not directly linked to food intolerance, there is no doubt that children can experience unpleasant symptoms when they are rundown or ill. It may be that a system under pressure is less likely to cope in the normal way with everyday foods and, as a result, symptoms develop. In this case, it is best to withdraw any food that causes a reaction until your child is back on form.

Some children may not have adequate amounts of some enzymes needed to digest certain foods. Insufficient quantities of the enzyme lactase, for example, make it difficult to digest lactose, the main sugar in milk products. Lactose intolerance can cause bloating, cramping, diarrhoea and excess gas (see pages 20–1). Furthermore, food poisoning can mimic an allergic reaction. Some types of mushrooms and rhubarb, for example, can be toxic. Bacteria in spoiled tuna and other fish can also produce a toxin that triggers adverse reactions.

There is also a peculiar psychological element to food intolerance. When a child is under pressure or has a particularly bad experience with a particular food (perhaps vomiting after eating too much, or their first taste coincided with a physical illness or a traumatic emotional event), they may actually develop something of a phobia, which results in the same symptoms occurring whenever that food is eaten. While the symptoms are undoubtedly psychosomatic, they are very real and it can be very difficult to ascertain whether there is a genuine intolerance, or the problem is simply a physical manifestation of an emotional problem.

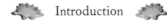

Introduction

11

Food intolerances can be very difficult to pinpoint, often because there may be more than one food implicated. Most children who are food intolerant are sensitive to between one and five foods, although older children whose intolerances have gone undiagnosed for many years may be intolerant to many more (up to 20 or 30 in some cases). The issue is further complicated by the fact that many children are intolerant or allergic to ingredients in a particular food, or something used in its processing, rather than the food itself. Ingredients that appear regularly in everyday foods and are recognized as common triggers include lactose, wheat, MSG (monosodium glutamate), salicylates and sulphites. A number of E-numbers (food additives) can create the same problem. In particular, watch out for tartrazine or E102, which has been linked to allergies in a number of people.

Symptoms of intolerance

Symptoms are often difficult to pinpoint, largely because they can seem innocuous in the early stages. The time it takes for symptoms to appear can also make it harder to link a reaction with a specific food. Some children become intolerant after a course of antibiotics, or being exposed to pesticides or other toxins. Symptoms may become worse in periods of stress, or after illness, which also clouds the issue.

Some of the most common symptoms include:

ANXIETY

ASTHMA

BEDWETTING IN CHILDREN OVER THE AGE OF
    THREE OR FOUR (ALTHOUGH THIS HAS
    OTHER CAUSES, INCLUDING EMOTIONAL
    FACTORS)

BEHAVIOURAL PROBLEMS

BLOATING

CHRONIC SNIFFLING

CONSTIPATION

COUGHING

CROHN'S DISEASE

DIARRHOEA

ECZEMA

EXCESS MUCUS

FACIAL PUFFINESS

FATIGUE

FLATULENCE

HEADACHES

HIVES

IBS

INDIGESTION

INSOMNIA

ITCHY EYES

ITCHY SKIN

MOOD SWINGS

MOUTH ULCERS

MUSCULAR ACHES

NAUSEA

SKIN RASHES (AROUND THE MOUTH,
    PARTICULARLY, ALTHOUGH THE WHOLE
    BODY MAY BE AFFECTED)

SORE THROATS

WATER RETENTION

WHEEZING

The best way to test for intolerance is to look for any changes in your child's health, even if it has been a slow progressive change. Does your child complain of headaches or excessive fatigue after meals? Does he get inexplicable skin rashes, particularly around his mouth? Is his behaviour worse after a particular type of food? Does he crave a particular type of food constantly? Does he have a constantly runny nose or sniffle?

Cravings are one of the key symptoms of intolerance. Some studies show that at least 50 per cent of us suffer food cravings for problem foods. We may even be unaware of it. Take a look at your own diet and see what foods you eat most commonly. Try cutting out these foods for several weeks and see if you experience better health to any significant degree. Many people who suffer from regular headaches, low-grade niggling health problems and fatigue are intolerant or sensitive to certain foods and it isn't until these foods are removed that they were even aware that a problem existed.

Look at the foods your child chooses, particularly if he or she is a picky eater. Children who refuse to eat anything other than peanut butter sandwiches, or pasta and cereal, for instance, show clear-cut tendencies for suspect foods.

The asthma connection

Some evidence suggests that food allergies and sensitivities can trigger asthma in older children, especially those with atopic dermatitis (eczema) or a history of eczema. In three different studies, asthmatic children cared for in pulmonary clinics were tested for food allergies. The children were screened for food allergies by history, skin testing and blood tests for IgE antibodies to foods. Any child suspected of having a food allergy was given a food challenge. Overall, 6–8 per cent of the children were found to have wheezing triggered during their food challenges. From these results, researchers concluded that food allergies contribute to asthma in less than 10 per cent of asthmatic children.

In another study of children with severe asthma and suspected food allergies, only one-quarter of the children were found to develop wheezing during double-blind food challenges. Less than 10 per cent of these children (2 per cent overall) developed wheezing as the only allergic symptom resulting from the food challenge.

The diagnosis of food-induced respiratory disease should be suspected if your child seems to develop wheezing within one to four hours after eating a certain food (especially if it happens on more than one occasion), if your child has atopic dermatitis or had a history of atopic dermatitis as an infant.

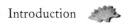

Is food intolerance connected with other childhood conditions?

- It is believed that food intolerance can cause or exacerbate such conditions as asthma, migraine, nasal congestion, eczema, hyperactivity, irritable bowel syndrome and Crohn's disease.
- One in 10 children has eczema and an estimated one in seven has asthma but exactly how many cases are linked to food is not known.
- Low-grade sensitivities can produce respiratory symptoms and children with chronic catarrh and/or recurrent colds and runny nose should be assessed for food intolerance.
- For the 22 per cent of those children with irritable bowel syndrome, the Allergy Research Foundation (ARF) believes a change in diet can help alleviate the problems in half of those cases.
- Evidence shows that 50 per cent of those suffering from Crohn's disease feel better when a particular food is eliminated from the diet.
- Frimley Children's Centre in the UK has used diet management to tackle a range of problems in children, including attention deficit disorder, irritable bowel syndrome and migraine.
- Professor Joseph Egger, professor of neurology at the Children's Hospital, Munich, has used brain mapping to illustrate the changes that take place in children suffering from attention deficit disorder after they have eaten certain foods, such as milk, chocolate and cereals.

Keeping a food diary

In order to work out a food or additive intolerance, you will need to keep a food diary of everything that passes your child's lips – not just meals, but also drinks, food supplements and even water. Record the time that each is eaten or drunk, the approximate quantities and relevant details, such as the brand and whether or not the food or drink is organic. Write all of these details on the left-hand page of a large notebook. On the right-hand page record any symptoms that you notice, the time they occur and how long they last. Obviously this is easier with older children, who will be able to tell you how they feel, or keep the diary themselves. With younger children you may want to note down any obvious changes in behaviour, any rashes or hives that might appear, and any changes in bowel movements, for example.

At the end of a week or so, go through the diary, looking for recurring patterns. You may notice that your child becomes slightly moody or hyperactive after eating toast or bread, or that he has a headache after eating a banana, or seems tired after a glass of milk, or complains of stomach pains after eating a cheese sandwich.

Make a comprehensive list of every food that seems to trigger a regular pattern of symptoms. Watch out too for foods that your child regularly craves, as these are likely to be the main culprits. If, at the end of about a week, you are no nearer to isolating the offending foods, an elimination diet can be considered.

Eliminating foods

Experts suggest that randomly withdrawing foods from a child's diet can be dangerous, leaving it unbalanced at a time when nutrients are required most. If you suspect a food allergy, keep a food diary for a week or two and if your child shows a reaction to a particular food, drop it completely. But take care to replace it in the diet with a food or group of foods with a similar nutrient content. For example, if you drop wheat or other gluten-containing foods, you must ensure that your child has another source of good-quality unrefined carbohydrates, as well as B vitamins, among other things.

Children need a varied diet and it is important not to cut out more than one or two foods at a time. If you cut out milk and milk products, for example, make sure your child is getting enough protein and calcium from other sources (plenty of green vegetables and pulses, for example). An elimination diet should have a fairly immediate effect, and you should notice that the symptoms are alleviated within a few days, certainly in the case of sensitivities and intolerance.

Elimination diets are a good idea for older children, while younger children should only undergo them with the supervision of a doctor or good qualified nutritionist. Allergies tend to focus on one food, or food group. Food intolerances, on the other hand, can be vast or they can be limited to just one or two key foods. Try the obvious ones first – for example, milk or wheat. If there is no obvious change in symptoms, introduce the foods back into the diet one at a time and try another suspect food, such as eggs, corn or oranges. In the case of suspected food allergies, rather than intolerance, you'll probably need to remove the danger food/s from your child's diet for a year or more. After this time your doctor will in all likelihood agree to a food challenge test to establish if the allergy still exists.

For children between the ages of two to four, with allergies to foods such as eggs, wheat or milk, a skin prick test will tell immediately if the offending food still causes a reaction. Allergies to shellfish and peanuts, which tend to be longer lasting, should not be tested until your child is at least seven. Some parents notice that a child has eaten the 'danger' food by accident, and has shown no sign of reacting. In these circumstances, you can try a small amount of the food a week or so later, or, better still, ask for another skin prick test in your doctor's office. Don't be tempted to reintroduce foods without checking that the allergy has

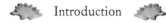

disappeared. Even well-prepared parents can be caught out by a severe reaction and that's not a risk any of us would want to take.

In the case of sensitivities and intolerance, you may be able to reintroduce foods much earlier – after a couple of months or even weeks. But take care to reintroduce foods one at a time and make a note of any symptoms that arise. Remember that symptoms may appear to be innocuous and not linked to diet, but take a good look at the possible symptoms on page 12, and watch out for them. If symptoms recur, drop the food again for another couple of months.

Preventing allergies and intolerance

There are a number of ways that allergies and intolerance can be prevented. According to recent research, babies can be sensitized to foods before they are born, because some food molecules from the food eaten by their mothers can reach the womb. The foods most likely to cause problems are often those craved by women while they were pregnant, or foods that were eaten in large quantities. Although milk can be a sensitivity factor for many babies, it is not the only one by far – so don't simply assume that it is the cause of the problem.

The most important thing you can do for your child is to undertake a preventative weaning programme, which involves carefully planning your child's diet to avoid potential allergens. With allergies on the increase, all children will benefit from this type of approach, as it greatly reduces the chances of even mild sensitivities setting in.

Breastfeeding is the best start to any child's life and although some women find this difficult, it is worth persevering – at least for the first couple of months. There are many undoubted benefits to breastfeeding but, in terms of allergies, it is important to consider the following:

- Breast milk is designed to provide complete nourishment for a baby for several months after its birth. Before milk is produced the mother's breast produces colostrum, a deep-yellow liquid containing high levels of protein and antibodies. A newborn baby who feeds on colostrum in the first few days of life is better able to resist the bacteria and viruses that cause illness. This is relevant for several reasons. First of all, when a baby is protected to some degree from potential illness, his immune system will not be under pressure and it will, therefore, be less likely to react in abnormal ways to food. Secondly, because proteins are implicated in so many food allergies and intolerance cases, it is important that babies receive the most natural and digestible form, which is found in human milk.
- The fat contained in human milk, compared with cow's milk (which most infant formulas are based on), is more digestible for babies and allows for greater absorption of fat-soluble vitamins into the bloodstream from the baby's intestine. Food allergies and intolerance are linked to deficiencies of a number of key nutrients – in particular, EFAs (essential fatty acids), which are present in human milk, but not in most infant formulas.

- Antigens in cow's milk can cause allergic reactions in a newborn baby, whereas such reactions to human milk are rare. Furthermore, other research has shown that breast-feeding for the first 15 weeks protects against diarrhoeal diseases. This is significant from the point of view that gut dysfunction appears to be related to food intolerance and sensitivity.

It is worth noting that food molecules are also transmitted via breast milk, which makes the breast-feeding mother's diet all-important in the fight against allergies. Ensure that you eat any potential allergens in moderation, particularly if there are allergies in the family, and try to eat as varied a diet as possible. Not only will your baby have a greater chance of getting the nutrients it needs, but you will also ensure that it is not in contact with any one potentially allergenic food in high levels.

If you can't breast-feed, it is important to choose your baby's formula with great care. Everything on the market will be safe, with balanced nutrients and added vitamins, although you may need to choose between brands according to your baby's age and special requirements. Most formulas are based on cow's milk, but there are soya-based formulas available for babies who have difficulty digesting cow's milk, or who have allergies or intolerance. However, these may also cause problems (see below).

You can also get a goat's milk preparation, although some babies do not like the pronounced taste. Watch out for baby formulas with GM ingredients (see page 39). If possible, go for an organic formula, which will hold far less risk in the long term (see pages 35–6).

Is soya milk the answer?

In some quarters, soya milk and other soya products have been heralded as the answer to food allergies and sensitivities. There are, however, many differing views on this approach and it is worth taking them into consideration when adding soya to your child's diet:

- Overeating or drinking any one food can lead to sensitivities and intolerance. In fact, infants allergic to cow's milk are, in 40–50 per cent of cases, also at risk of developing an allergy to soya.
- Before replacing cow's milk with soya milk in your child's diet, read the labels carefully. Soya milk is not naturally high in calcium, which children need to build strong bones. Look for a soya milk fortified with calcium, and choose an organic brand if you can find it.
- Soya is a food product that has been heavily involved in genetic modification. Ensure that any soya product you purchase is GM free and preferably organic.
- Soya is a prime source of phyto-oestrogens, which are natural compounds that act as weak oestrogens. While phyto-oestrogens have been shown to have a positive effect on the

health of adults (they may offer some protection against conditions such as breast, bowel, prostate and other cancers, cardiovascular disease and menopausal symptoms), there are concerns over the long-term effects of phyto-oestrogens given to infants and young children, largely on the grounds that they can play havoc with hormonal activity.

- Currently, breast milk or cow's milk formula are recommended for infant feeding, unless there is a clear indication that soya milk formula is required on medical grounds. One answer might be to choose a good organic soya formula for the first six months of life and then switch to an organic cow's or goat's milk formula for the next six months, or until weaning is complete.

First foods

When you choose to wean your child will also have an impact on their susceptibility to allergies. Research very clearly shows that leaving first foods as late as possible will help to ensure that your child's digestive system is mature enough to cope. Six months is a reasonable time to start with a little table food – some rice, a few fruits and vegetables, for example, but leave it longer if you can, particularly if there are allergies of any nature in your family. Don't be tempted to replace all milk in a baby's diet. Until your baby is about a year old, she will get most of her nutrition from milk. Other foods will add a little variety and introduce her to new tastes, but they should not be relied upon as a source of a balanced diet. Early foods merely supplement milk feeds, so there is no reason to worry if your baby has nothing but milk for the first six or seven months of life.

Some babies will thrive on milk for the first 12 months, so don't panic if you have a slow beginner. If you wish to stop breast-feeding, you can switch to the bottle long before you need to give solid foods. Similarly, it is not advised that you give solid foods to a baby that is younger than three months. It is now believed that babies' digestive systems are not mature enough to cope with solids before this time, and they will be more prone to food allergies, rashes and digestive upsets.

There are foods that should not be introduced too early in any child's diet – whether or not there are allergies in the family. Try to stick to these basic guidelines:

- First foods should be introduced one at a time and any reactions noted (see page 12).
- Do not give children eggs, fish, chocolate, wheat, orange, peanuts or other nuts for at least the first six months, or preferably for the first year of life. These are the most common allergens. (Eggs means any birds' eggs – they all contain similar proteins and are best regarded as a single food item.)
- Tomatoes, aubergines, potatoes and peppers should also not form a part of a baby's diet until his first birthday. These vegetables are members of the 'nightshade' family of vegetables, which contain toxins that are now being linked to a variety of health conditions, including

headaches and depression. Your child may not be susceptible to the toxins contained in these vegetables, but it is wise to play safe.

- Test out beef and eggs cautiously. Beef can cross-react with milk (they're from the same source) and chicken's eggs can cross-react with chicken itself. If they seem to cause no problems, include them in your child's diet.
- Infant formulas commonly contain maize (corn) and tapioca, as well as cow's milk, so there is a possibility that your child has become sensitive to these foods. Avoid including them in your child's diet until he is at least nine months old (and watch out for hidden ingredients – corn, for example, is found in cornflour, corn oil, corn syrup, popcorn and cornflakes).
- Some grains containing gluten, such as oats, rye and barley, can be introduced at about a year, but resist giving your child wheat until they are between a year and two years of age (in other words, as long as possible).
- Soya products and ground nuts and seeds can be introduced, one by one, at about a year, but make sure you try them out, one at a time, and watch carefully for any reaction.
- Dairy products, such as cow's milk, cheese and yogurt, citrus fruits and eggs can be introduced singly after a year, but, again, leave them as long as possible.
- Shellfish and strawberries can be introduced when your child is two years old.
- Whole nuts should not form part of your child's diet until at least the age of five. Quite apart from the possibility of allergies, nuts are responsible for an alarming number of deaths caused by choking.
- No food should be eaten in large quantities and it is a good idea to avoid giving any one food on a daily basis. This does mean being imaginative with your child's diet, but if you try to eat a varied diet as a family, it should be easier to achieve. Try out fruits, vegetables and grains that you may not normally consider buying: sweet potatoes, kale, pulses (such as lentils and black beans), dried unsulphured fruits soaked and puréed, millet, rice, parsnips, kiwi fruit, mango, quinoa, chickpeas (garbanzos), buckwheat, split peas, barley and tofu.

The cautious approach has been proved through a variety of different studies aimed at helping to prevent allergies and intolerance in susceptible children. For example, Dr Zeiger's investigation (see page 6) followed 165 children from birth to age seven who were at high risk of developing allergies because of their parents' allergic conditions. He concluded: 'Avoiding the early introduction of potentially allergenic foods is the basic step in the primary prevention of food allergies in children who are at high risk, but some infants may still become sensitized or allergic to a food. Signs of food allergy in infants include eczema, hives, wheezing, or vomiting from formula. Fortunately, early detection of a food allergy can help reduce its severity.'

Interestingly, Zeiger also found that children with food allergies are several times more likely to develop a respiratory allergy as they get older. He noted that the earlier we can identify food and other allergic conditions, the earlier we can step in to prevent allergic disorders such as asthma and allergic rhinitis.

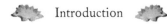 Introduction

When you begin introducing foods, those least likely to cause allergic reactions should be introduced first. These include rice and rice cereals (although watch out for added milk), pear, apple and carrots. Other good first foods include peaches, apricots, bananas (it is worth noting that very ripe bananas improve the health of the gut, which can be crucial for those susceptible to food allergies), parsnips, swede, green beans, squash, sweet potato, cauliflower, peas and broccoli. Introduce them separately, about a week apart, and keep the diet as varied as possible.

Understanding the problems

The symptoms of allergies and intolerance vary between sufferers and unless your child has a full-blown anaphylactic reaction to a certain food, you may not be sure whether or not food is at the root of any problems. However, many of the main allergies and intolerances share certain features in common. In this section, we'll examine each of the main sensitivities, their characteristics and how you can give your child the best possible chance of overcoming their condition.

Lactose intolerance

Lactose is the main sugar found in milk (and therefore all dairy products). When a child is lactose intolerant, it simply means that they are unable to digest this type of sugar, largely because of a shortage of a digestive enzyme called lactase, which is normally produced in the small intestine. Lactase is responsible for breaking down milk sugar in order that it can be absorbed into the bloodstream. When there is not enough lactase available to digest lactose, the child will experience often very painful symptoms. Most commonly, these include nausea, cramps, bloating, diarrhoea and gas; these symptoms normally occur between 30 minutes and 2 hours after eating or drinking foods containing lactose. Symptoms do vary in severity, depending on how intolerant the child is, or in other words, how much lactase is being produced in the intestine.

There is undoubtedly an ethnic link to this condition and Westernized Africans and Asians tend to be the hardest hit, with as many as 90 per cent suffering. However, irrespective of ethnicity, lactase is produced in decreasing quantities after the age of about two years, although symptoms may not occur until much later in life. Some babies are actually born without the ability to produce lactase, which makes feeding difficult. Other causes include digestive disorders, injuries to the small intestine and even repeated courses of antibiotics, which destroy the healthy intestinal bacteria (known as flora) and upset the intestine's ability to produce lactase.

There are a variety of different tests used to diagnose this condition, including breath tests, stool acidity and blood tests. These are not, however, recommended for young children. If symptoms are present, it is commonly agreed that withdrawal of all dairy produce is the best course of action. Young children with lactase deficiency should therefore not eat any foods containing lactose. Older children can often manage small quantities, but acceptable levels will differ. It is really just a question of trying out different foods to ascertain which cause the most problems.

It is also possible to purchase lactase enzymes over the counter, and these come in a variety of different forms. Drops, for example, can be added to milk and left for 24 hours, after which the lactose content is reduced significantly. Other forms include chewable tablets, which are taken just before any food that contains lactose. It is also worth looking out for lactose-reduced dairy products (in particular, milk and yogurt), which contain the same levels of nutrients as brands with the normal levels of lactose.

Alternative sources of nutrients

The main nutrients contained in milk and other dairy products include protein, lots of calcium, some B vitamins and a little iron. Full-fat milk also contains vitamins A, D and E. All round, it is a good nutritious fast food for children, but it is not, despite advertisements to the contrary, essential.

Leafy green vegetables are an excellent source of calcium, in particular broccoli and kale, and fish with soft, edible bones, such as salmon (canned is fine), whitebait and sardines, are also an excellent option. Recent research shows that yogurt with active cultures may be a good source of calcium for many people with lactose intolerance, although it is fairly high in lactose. It appears that the bacterial cultures used in making yogurt produce some of the lactase enzyme required for proper digestion. It also helps to improve the health of the intestine, which ensures normal function and better absorption of nutrients. Vitamin A is also found in most brightly coloured vegetables (as beta carotene) and in meats, eggs, liver and fish liver oil. Vitamin D is also found in eggs, fish liver oils and most fish. Soya, vegetable oils, leafy green vegetables and eggs will also provide adequate amounts of vitamin E.

Supplements may be appropriate if your child is a finicky eater, but it is worth seeing a good qualified nutritionist or dietician to ensure that quantities are correct for his or her individual needs. All children will benefit from a good multi-vitamin and mineral tablet.

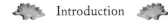

Milk allergy

Having a milk allergy is not the same as being lactose intolerant. Instead of being unable to digest lactose, a child suffering from a milk allergy has a reaction to the *protein* in milk. It is possible to be sensitive to or intolerant of the proteins in milk, as well as being lactose intolerant. In such circumstances, it is best to avoid dairy produce altogether. A milk allergy is, of course, also an allergy to dairy products – that means anything that comes from a cow.

According to research, sufferers fall into three main categories in terms of their response to the proteins in milk. The first group reacts immediately, within 45 minutes of drinking cow's milk or a product containing it. Symptoms in this group normally include urticaria (hives), swelling and anaphylaxis. The second group responds more slowly, taking anything between 45 minutes and 20 hours to exhibit symptoms. These include pallor, vomiting and diarrhoea. The third group takes longer than 20 hours to respond, and symptoms include skin, respiratory and gut reactions. A true milk (dairy) allergy involves a histamine reaction (see page 3), and indicates that your child's body sees the proteins in dairy produce as an invader, thereby setting up an immune response against them.

Milk is used in a wide variety of different foods and is listed on the label under various names. Once again, it is crucial that you take time to read the labels, to ensure that milk isn't an extra hidden ingredient. Look out for:

CASEIN

CASEINATE

WHEY

WHEY POWDER

SODIUM CASEINATE

CALCIUM CASEINATE

CARAMEL (ALTHOUGH AS A PURE UNADULTERATED COLOUR, THIS IS ALL RIGHT)

Milk proteins are found in:

CHEESE

YOGURT

BUTTER

MOST MARGARINES

CUSTARD

BISCUITS

CAKES

MANY BREADS (INCLUDING BREADCRUMBS)

MOST CHOCOLATES

SOME BRANDS OF CANNED TUNA

Goat's milk protein is similar to cow's milk protein and may, therefore, cause a reaction in milk-allergic individuals. The same goes for sheep's milk. Soya seems to be the best alternative, although it has problems of its own (see page 17). The best approach is to ensure that your child is getting the nutrients he may be missing in a dairy-free diet (see page 21), and use soya products sparingly in the interim. It may well be that your child will outgrow his or her allergy.

Wheat allergy

Once again, it is possible to be allergic to the proteins in wheat and/or intolerant or simply sensitive to wheat itself. The enthusiasm for whole grains and dietary fibre over the past decade has lead to a general tendency to overeat grains – in particular, wheat. Therefore, many cases of intolerance and sensitivity are due more to overconsumption than a true allergy.

The protein in wheat is gluten, which is also found in other cereal grains, such as rye, oats and barley. Those with coeliac disease or 'coeliac sprue' suffer from an adverse reaction to gluten. It is a permanent condition and sufferers almost never lose their sensitivity to this substance. The only treatment is lifelong restriction of gluten – and that means any of the grains that contain it. In contrast, those who have a wheat allergy (an immune-mediated response to wheat protein) must avoid only wheat. Confusing, it is, but there are differences

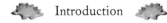 Introduction 23

between the gluten found in the various grains, and studies show that wheat-allergic people can normally eat other gluten-containing grains without any problem. Most wheat-allergic children outgrow the allergy.

The exact cause of coeliac disease is unknown. It develops in children (and adults) who are genetically predisposed to the condition, and occurs when eating grains containing gluten. Some children do not develop the disease until a trigger, such as a viral illness or in some cases immunization, begins the abnormal immune response. Coeliac disease causes the intestine to lose its ability to absorb nutrients, hence weight loss, anaemia and vitamin deficiencies may occur as a result of exposure to gluten. Intestinal damage may also develop within a few months and may not become evident for several years.

Because the exact cause is unknown, there is no way of preventing the development of coeliac disease. However, awareness of risk factors (such as a family member with the disorder) may increase the chance of early diagnosis and treatment. Total withdrawal of gluten from the diet permits the intestinal mucosa to heal and results in a disappearance of the symptoms of the disease. Initially, irritability subsides and appetite improves, usually within a matter of days following withdrawal of dietary gluten.

Although wheat-intolerant or -allergic children are not restricted to the same extent as coeliacs, it can still be difficult to provide them with a 'normal' diet, as so many 'kid-friendly' foods contain wheat or other grains. Popular breakfast cereals, ordinary bread, cereal bars, biscuits, cakes and many other staples are off the menu, but the recipes in this book should provide perfect alternatives to all of your child's favourite foods.

Recent studies have shown that wheat-intolerant children may actually be allergic or sensitive to the pesticide residues in wheat. Wheat is one of the most heavily sprayed crops in the world and because the grain is so small, large quantities of pesticides can be absorbed. Some families have found that switching to organic wheat products has resulted in their children's allergies and sensitivities disappearing.

Avoiding wheat and gluten

Becoming wheat free means eliminating all products that might contain wheat, whilst becoming gluten free requires removing all products that might contain wheat and other offending grains such as rye, oats and barley. It is important to carefully read all product labels because products labelled wheat free are not necessarily gluten free.

Watch out for these terms. Every one of these foods is a type of wheat:

DURUM FLOUR

COUSCOUS

SEMOLINA

KAMUT

BULGUR

TRITICALE

SPELT

The following products may also contain gluten:

STARCH

DEXTRIN

MALT

MALTODEXTRIN

HVP (HYDROLYSED VEGETABLE PROTEIN)

FILLERS

NATURAL FLAVOURINGS

CHEWING GUM (IT IS OFTEN DUSTED WITH WHEAT FLOUR TO PREVENT STICKINESS)

Alternative sources of nutrients

Grains are an extremely good source of many vital nutrients, including the B vitamins, vitamin E, zinc, magnesium and healthy proteins, and these must be replaced in a child's diet in order to ensure a good balance of nutrients.

Vegetables contain good levels of the B-complex vitamins, as does wholegrain rice, fish, eggs, dairy produce, yeast, molasses and seeds. The problem is, of course, that many children are sensitive to eggs and dairy produce, which can limit intake substantially. The best option is to take a good multi-vitamin and mineral tablet containing the B-complex vitamins, and ensure that a variety of different vegetables are eaten on a daily basis – easier said than done in some cases! Marmite is high in B vitamins, as are many pulses (although these can also present problems), and whole rice should be eaten several times a day.

Magnesium is another key nutrient and because it is implicated in many cases of false food allergy (see page 8), it may be that supplementation – as well as ensuring good dietary levels – can help to rectify multiple food sensitivities in children. Good natural sources include figs, lemons, grapefruit, sweetcorn, almonds, nuts, seeds, dark green vegetables and apples – most of which are, happily, very child friendly. Zinc is found in lamb, beef, pork, yeast, pumpkin seeds, eggs, non-fat dry milk and nuts, and is essential for immunity.

Egg allergy

Egg allergy is one of the most common food allergies in babies and young children, although it is also almost always outgrown by the age of about five. Once again, proteins are at the root of this allergy. The four main allergenic proteins in egg – ovalbumin, ovomucoid, ovotransfferin and lysozyme – are contained in the egg white. Ovalbumin, the major allergen, comprises about half of the egg white. While most children are allergic to proteins in the egg white, some

 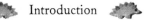

are allergic to the yolk. There are three yolk proteins that tend to cause problems, but allergies to these are less common in children.

In some children, the reaction is triggered by inhaled bird antigens – a condition known as bird-egg syndrome. Interestingly, egg allergies can be also be seasonal. Children who suffer from some types of hay fever may experience a reaction to eggs when some pollens are in season.

The symptoms associated with egg allergy include allergic rhinitis, asthma, dermatitis, diarrhoea, gastrointestinal symptoms, hives, nausea, vomiting, wheezing and, in some cases, anaphylaxis.

Eggs are, unfortunately, found in a huge number of products, including baked goods, sauces, breaded meats, cereals, flours, sweets, biscuits, custards, noodles, desserts, fondants, some processed meats, ice cream, pasta, malted drinks, mayonnaise, meringues, soups, salad dressings, sausages, pancakes and even some wines. In addition, many breads and baked goods are brushed with egg to provide an attractive finish. Even worse, many cosmetics, including shampoos, contain egg proteins, so be sure to read the labels carefully.

What to look out for

Eggs are listed under a plethora of different terms and parents of egg-allergic or -sensitive children will need to be aware of them all. Watch out for:

ALBUMIN

GLOBULIN

LIVETIN

LYSOZYME

OVALBUMIN

OVOGLOBULIN

OVOMUCIN

OVOMUCOID

OVOTRANSFERRIN

OVOVITELIA

OVOVITELLIN

SILICI ALBUMINATE

SIMPLESSE

VITELLIN

Lecithin may also be made with egg yolks.

Alternative sources of nutrients

Eggs are a good source of first-class protein and contain B-vitamins (especially B12), as well as many other nutrients, including zinc, vitamins A, D and E, and lecithin, a mineral that is necessary for the metabolic processes of the body.

  Allergy-Free Cooking for Kids

Animal products such as meat, yogurt, milk and butter are a good alternative to eggs and will provide much-needed protein, as well as vitamin B12, vitamin A and D and zinc. Whole grains, legumes, seeds and brightly coloured vegetables are also good sources of many of the vital nutrients found in eggs.

Peanut allergy

Peanut allergy is on the increase and is the source of great concern for manufacturers and consumers alike. The simple reason is that peanuts can be deadly to a small percentage of the population and accidental contact or even inhalation of peanut particles can cause a severe allergic reaction that can lead to anaphylaxis.

The peanut is a member of the legume family and is not considered to be a true nut. A peanut allergy is one of the most common food allergies because the proteins in peanuts can act as powerful allergens, even in tiny quantities, and with minimal contact.

Children under the age of three are most likely to have food sensitivities, probably because their immune systems cannot yet tolerate a wide range of new substances. Therefore, children with a family history of food allergies should not be given peanuts or peanut products until at least the age of three, and preferably later.

Although once considered to be a life-long allergy, recent studies indicate that up to 20 per cent of children diagnosed with peanut allergy outgrow it. For the others, the allergy will be life-long. Peanuts can cause reactions ranging from itching or swelling of the lips, tongue, or mouth, to life-threatening shortness of breath and a drop in blood pressure.

Avoidance is obviously the main way to manage a peanut allergy and parents must be scrupulous to ensure that children do not come into contact with anything that has even minute traces of peanuts or peanut butter. The oil from peanuts tends to linger, so it is also important that cooking, serving and even play equipment does not contain traces.

Labelling has improved so it should now be clear if there are peanuts or other nuts contained within a product, but look out for terms such as peanut extract, ground nuts, mixed nuts, or natural flavouring. Arachis oil is, in fact, peanut oil. Processed foods, such as baked goods, sweets, cereals, cookies, dips, egg rolls, chocolates, ice cream and pasta sauces may contain hidden peanuts. African, Chinese, Indonesian, Mexican, Thai and Vietnamese dishes often contain peanuts, so it is best to avoid these cuisines, both in the supermarket (as contamination of ready-made meals could have occurred even if peanuts are not used in that specific meal) and in restaurants. Read all labels carefully.

Other nuts and nut butters may be fine for your child, but most experts recommend avoiding all tree nuts if there is a nut allergy, if only because they are processed, packaged or produced on equipment used for peanuts.

If your child is allergic to peanuts, be sure that everyone who feeds and cares for the child knows about the allergy and what to do in the event of an attack. Parents should teach allergic

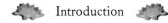

children to ask about food they are offered. Most experts believe that banning peanuts at school is not advisable, as it promotes a false sense of security and teaches children nothing about dealing with allergies in the real world. Although there is always a risk of contamination, for instance from playground equipment or in the dining hall, there will be risks throughout their lives and children need to learn to cope.

It is vitally important that all peanut allergic patients have an action plan in place to deal quickly with an accidental ingestion of peanuts. Most doctors recommend giving children an epinephrine (adrenaline) 'pen', which should be carried and used in an emergency. Teachers, babysitters, carers and even parents of your child's friends should be given a pen to use in an emergency.

Other nut allergies

Tree nut allergies are also, inexplicably, on the increase – perhaps because they are so prevalent in processed foods and also found in the vast majority of foods children most like.

Tree nuts include cashews, almonds, pecans, pistachios, macadamia and walnuts, among others. Some children do have an allergy to both peanuts and tree nuts. It is safest to avoid all kinds of nuts even if your child is allergic to just one. The processing of nuts in foods lends itself to cross-contamination and it may not be a risk you are prepared to take. Any product that says 'nuts' must be avoided, including oils, butters and pastes.

Tree nuts are used in many foods, including barbecue sauces, cereals, biscuits and cookies, ice cream and even flavoured crisps. Many extruded snacks (those that contain a variety of processed ingredients) also contain them. Natural and artificial flavourings may be based on tree nuts and even some cheeses contain traces used for flavouring.

It is worth noting that coconuts are not considered to be tree nuts and are therefore normally safe. However, as a high-fat food with few nutrients and even less fibre, it is not ideal or essential for children and is best used in small amounts for flavouring savoury and sweet dishes.

Alternative sources of nutrients

Nuts are an excellent source of protein and most of the B-complex vitamins. Almonds, for example, are rich in zinc, magnesium, potassium, iron, B vitamins and have very high levels of calcium. Seeds are a good alternative and most children love the taste, particularly when they are gently roasted. Try sunflower seeds, which provide large amounts of protein, B vitamins, iron, zinc, potassium and selenium, and are one of the best sources of vitamin E. Sesame seeds are an exceptional source of calcium and a very good source of protein and magnesium. They are also rich in B vitamins, especially niacin and folate. Sesame seeds are traditionally used to make tahini, a thick paste that is similar in texture to peanut butter and just as nutritious.

Shellfish and fish allergies

Allergic reactions to fish and shellfish are common in many children. Generally speaking, an allergy to shellfish does not suggest a similar allergy to fish, but in some children both allergies occur. As a rule of thumb, a fish allergy precludes eating *any* type of fish, just as an allergy to one type of shellfish means that *all* types should be avoided.

Fish allergies tend to be highest where fish is eaten frequently. In Sweden, for example, around 39 per cent of children are allergic to fish. The figure has been rising over a number of years, which may be linked to the fact that more and more fish is farmed, fish products are used increasingly in processed foods, and the processing of fish itself has changed, with milk solutions being used instead of water, thereby adding in more potential allergens. In general, about 22 per cent of the population is allergic or sensitive to fish.

Fish allergies are more common in children, whereas shellfish allergies tend to affect more adults. After eggs and milk, seafood is the third leading cause of food allergy. It is an allergy that does not usually go away or diminish with age – it usually lasts a lifetime with the reactions becoming more severe with each subsequent exposure.

The fish that are implicated most often in allergies include cod, salmon, trout, herring, sardines, bass, orange roughy, swordfish, halibut and tuna. Shellfish commonly known to cause allergic reactions include shrimp, prawns, crab, crayfish, lobster, oysters, clams, scallops, mussels and squid. (Snails, although not classed as seafood, are part of the mollusc family and hence can cause similar problems.) Prawns appear to be the worst offender, causing respiratory problems in most sufferers; crab is also a powerful allergen to many children. Common symptoms include skin, stomach, or respiratory problems. More specifically they can include nasal congestion, hives, itching, swelling, wheezing or shortness of breath, nausea, upset stomach, cramps, heartburn, gas, diarrhoea, light-headedness, or fainting. Reactions usually appear within two hours of ingestion, inhaling cooking vapours, or handling. However, it has been reported the reactions can be delayed as long as 24 hours.

A number of highly processed foods may contain hidden fish or shellfish, so read food labels carefully. For example, the basis for imitation crab, lobster and prawns is pollock. It can also be used in beef and pork substitutes as part of hot dogs, ham, and pizza toppings. Fish skin is used to clarify some coffees and wines, while other parts of fish are used in Worcestershire sauce, many Asian meals, Caesar salad, salad dressings, cooking sauces and much, much more.

Alternative sources of nutrients

Fish and shellfish are an excellent source of protein. Fish, in particular, is a rich source of vitamin A, vitamin D, omega-3 fatty acids (an essential fatty acid required for learning, growth and development in children, and also linked to immunity and preventing allergies) and calcium. Shellfish are high in selenium and iron.

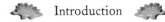 Introduction

29

It is the essential fatty acids, or EFAs, found in fish that are most important for children, but these can be easily replaced by drizzling flaxseed oil over meals and adding plenty of fresh seeds to the diet. If your child is fussy, try toasting the seeds or grinding them into a paste and stirring into casseroles and sauces.

Selenium is an important mineral, but it also is found in good quantities in onions, tomatoes, broccoli and wheatgerm. Iron is also crucial for growing children and a surprising number of children are anaemic, which underlines the need to ensure that your child has a good intake of this mineral. Iron is found in organ meats, dried fruits (in particular peaches), egg yolks, nuts, beans, asparagus, molasses and oatmeal.

Allergies to additives and preservatives

Food processing has increased a great deal over the past couple of decades and there are now literally hundreds of additives used regularly in children's food. Many experts believe that these chemicals place an extra strain on immature systems, resulting in children that are more susceptible to allergies in the present and perhaps laying down the foundation for allergies in the future.

Two widely-used additives – MSG and sulphites – are a particular cause for concern. MSG (monosodium glutamate) is a food additive that enhances flavour by stimulating the taste buds. After MSG was linked to brain damage in infant laboratory animals in 1970, manufacturers agreed to stop adding it to baby food. But MSG is still commonly added to many products, including canned soup, convenience foods, flavoured crisps, fried chicken batter and Chinese food. Foods that are chemically close enough to MSG, and thought to produce similar reactions, include hydrolysed vegetable protein and yeast extract. Symptoms of MSG sensitivity include dizziness, nausea, skin rash, migraine headache, asthma-type symptoms, flushing and tremors.

Sulphites are sometimes used to preserve the colour of foods such as dried fruits and vegetables, and to inhibit the growth of micro-organisms in fermented foods such as wine. Whilst sulphites are safe for most people, a small segment of the population has been found to develop shortness of breath, or even fatal shock, shortly after exposure to these preservatives. Sulphites are capable of producing severe asthma attacks in sulphite-sensitive asthmatics.

Although all additives go through rigorous testing, in combination they may prove to be a deadly cocktail. Most of the chemicals in our foods are 'anti-nutrients', in that they stop nutrients being absorbed and used. These crucial nutrients are the same ones that keep our children healthy, encourage healthy development and growth, and prevent illnesses such as cancer and heart disease.

Not only are food additives a major cause of health problems, but they can play havoc with an immature system, affecting growth, mood, concentration, sleeping patterns and overall resistance to infection by overloading your child's system with toxins. Children's food is full of some of the worst additives, largely because manufacturers know that something brightly coloured, over-sweetened or processed to look like a favourite cartoon character is more likely to appeal to a faddy child. Fight back by educating yourself about this problem, reading labels and avoiding the junk whenever possible. The recipes in this book are all free of additives, representing not only a safe option for allergic children, but a much healthier option for all children.

What children really need

All children require a healthy diet based on fresh, whole foods, but it is even more important if your child suffers from allergies. The aim is to provide foods that heal and provide the optimum level of nutrients for development, growth, immunity and the efficient functioning of all body systems. If your child's digestion is working well, for example, he will be much more likely to absorb the nutrients he needs from his food. And because so many allergies are related to gut function, it is even more important that your child eats foods that will enhance the health of the gut.

The key is obviously to improve our children's diets – by replacing processed foods with natural, unrefined alternatives. Our children need to eat more fruits and vegetables, whole grains, pulses, lean meats and low-fat dairy produce. This will make a dramatic difference to their overall health. Reduce or remove anything with artificial chemicals, in the form of additives, preservatives, flavours and anything else. All of these put a strain on the body, in particular the liver, which is so crucial for detoxification and healthy digestion. What's more, these chemicals are a form of environmental pollution, which will raise your child's toxic load and therefore burden his or her system further.

Given that digestion can be compromised in the case of allergies, and because your child's diet may be necessarily limited, it is important that the food your child eats contains the best possible combination of nutrients. At the very least you can then be confident that what your child is eating is contributing to health and growth, rather than detracting from it.

The next step is to offer supplements to balance some of the unhealthy aspects of our children's diets and to redress some of the damage caused by poor eating habits. Many children are faddy eaters, despite their parents' best efforts to provide good, nutritious meals, and they are at an increased risk of vitamin and mineral deficiencies. Every child past the stage of breast-feeding needs a good multi-vitamin and mineral tablet. (Even if a child has a very good diet, our nutrient-poor soil means that crops are often lacking in nutrients.)

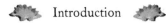

Aim for the following:

- Lots of healthy proteins, including very lean meats, fish, poultry, cheese, yogurt, nuts, soya products (including tofu), pulses such as lentils, and seeds (3–5 servings a day).
- Plenty of fruit and vegetables and their juices. Anything goes. Remember that the more colourful the vegetable, the more nutritious it tends to be (5–7 servings a day).
- Lots of carbohydrates for energy. Choose wholegrain or unrefined options, including pastas, bread, brown rice, grains (such as rye, barley, corn, buckwheat), pulses, potatoes and wholegrain, sugar-free cereals (4–9 servings a day)
- As much fluid as your child can drink. Water is the most important – between 0.5 and 2 litres (2–8 cups) is recommended, depending on age and weather.
- Choose fibre-rich foods, to help encourage digestion and optimum uptake of nutrients from the food they eat.
- Eat organic whenever possible (see page 35). There is still considerable debate about whether or not it is more nutritious, but there is no doubt that it is lower in chemicals that place strain on your child's system.
- Cut down on sweets, crisps, soft drinks and fast or 'junk' foods of any nature. These not only tend to take the place of healthier alternatives in our children's diets but they are also a key source of damaging chemicals and 'anti-nutrients'.
- Watch the sugar (see box below)

A healthy diet doesn't mean monotonous, tasteless meals. Experiment with a variety of different herbs and spices and try out new things to tempt your child. Get them involved in choosing menus and preparing the food. Let them know why you are eating particular foods and how it will make them feel better, do better on the sports field, or get over those constant colds. And don't worry about the odd slip-up. Life would be fairly joyless without the occasional naughty treat. As long as your child's diet is 80 per cent healthy, you don't need to worry too much about the other 20 per cent!

Why cut the sugar?

Virtually all of us have sugar occasionally – and it is particularly difficult to stop children eating it on a regular basis. However, you should be aware of the detrimental effect it has on the body. Sugar has a strong depressive effect on the immune system. According to a 1997 study, as little as 6 teaspoons a day can reduce the immune response by 25 per cent. Most common foods – particularly those geared towards children – contain a substantial amount of sugar, which can have a dramatic effect on our children's health. Children with allergies have a dysfunctional immune response and it is important that sugar is limited as much as possible, in order to ensure that their immune systems are working at optimum level.

Most importantly, however, the extra calories of sugars often displace more nourishing food in the diet. Diets high in sugar are also often high in fat and low in fibre. If your children fill up on sugary foods, they are likely to be at risk of the vitamin and mineral deficiencies that can underpin allergies in the first place.

Do children need supplements?

Ideally, a balanced, healthy diet contains foods that are high in all of the nutrients we need. However, vitamins are easily destroyed by canning, processing, refining and even cooking. Minerals are not necessarily present in foods – the quality of the soil and the geological conditions of the area in which they were grown play an important part in determining the mineral content of food. Even a balanced diet may be lacking in essential minerals or trace elements because of the soil in which the food was grown. There's pretty strong evidence that intensive farming robs soil of its nutrient content, which means that our food is naturally lower in minerals than it should be.

Secondly, and perhaps most importantly, our modern, overscheduled lives place demands on our bodies that cause them to require extra nutrients. Pollution, noise, stress, food additives and many other factors combine to put added stress on the body. Stress of any kind – whether it is emotional or physical – increases our need, and our children's need, for nutrients.

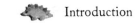

Supplementing your child's diet

- Every child will benefit from essential fatty acids (EFAs), now dangerously deficient in our diets. Essential fatty acids are converted into substances that keep our blood thin, lower blood pressure, decrease inflammation, improve the function of our nervous and immune systems, help insulin to work, encourage healthy metabolism, maintain the balance of water in our bodies and affect our vision, co-ordination and mood. There is also exciting new research showing that it can have a positive effect on children's behaviour and ability to learn. Try flaxseed oil (dribbled on foods or whizzed in the blender with orange juice), which is high in crucial omega-3 oils. Evening primrose oil, pumpkin seed oil and borage oil are also good sources of EFAs. A shortage of EFAs has also been linked to allergies.
- If your child has recurrent infections (colds, coughs and ear infections), make sure that he or she has extra vitamin C, which helps to boost the immune system. Constant, low-grade infections are a sign that the immune system is not functioning at optimum level. Give it a boost. Many experts recommend extra vitamin C as a matter of course, to help ward off illness. Between 100 and 1000mg is appropriate, depending on the child's age. A two-year-old, for example, might have an extra 100mg. If there is any diarrhoea after taking the tablets, reduce the dose by half.
- With iron-deficiency anaemia on the increase, it may be necessary to supplement iron. Most good vitamin and mineral tablets contain iron.
- Children who are unable to eat or drink dairy produce because of allergies, or because they simply don't like them, should be able to get enough calcium from vegetable and fruit sources. However, if you have a picky eater on your hands, you might need to consider calcium supplements.
- Zinc is crucial for children with allergies. It is needed for cell repair, efficient digestion, immune function and emotional health. About a third of all children do not get even the minimum suggested amount of zinc. Try a supplement of around 10–15mg per day.
- Because of the role of the gut in food allergies, an acidophilus tablet is recommended. These come in chewable, vanilla-flavoured tablets, or as capsules (which can be sprinkled over food). Acidophilus helps to restore the balance of healthy bacteria in the gut, which aids nutrient absorption, improves bowel health and ensures proper elimination.

Specific foods that help

A healthy diet is essential for good health and overall physical resilience. There are, however, other things that a food can do. Some foods have a direct effect on various organs or systems in the body and by increasing these foods in your child's diet, you'll be helping him to become stronger in areas where he might be most susceptible.

- Mango: Mangoes are rich in antioxidants and contain an acid that helps bowel health.
- Apricots: These are another good source of antioxidants. Fresh is best, but if you go for the dried version, make sure they are not sulphured.
- Bananas: Bananas contain potassium, which is required for nerve functioning and the health of the heart and brain. They help to keep blood pressure at a healthy level and encourage the action of the kidneys. Very ripe bananas also help to improve bowel health.
- Broccoli: An excellent source of magnesium, which is known to be deficient in the diets of many people with a food allergy.
- Nuts and seeds: These contain EFAs, as well as calcium and magnesium, which help to maintain a healthy nervous system, bones and teeth, and immunity. Nuts and seeds also contain zinc.
- Red onions: These contain several compounds that work in different ways. They are a good source of powerful antioxidants, but they also contain acids that support the liver and help to excrete toxins. Other properties include being antibiotic, anti-viral and anti-candida. Given that an allergic child's system is undoubtedly under pressure, these properties can greatly enhance health.
- Brown rice: A powerful detoxifier, brown rice has a soothing and cleansing effect on the digestive tract. It is also rich in the B vitamins, which are essential for nervous health.
- Oats: Not only are oats rich in B vitamins, important for a healthy nervous system, but they supply silicon for healthy arterial walls. What's more, they contain calcium, potassium and magnesium, all of which can be absent from, or low, in a restricted diet.
- Avocados: These are considered almost a complete food, supplying protein and carbohydrates as well as healthy fats. They are rich in potassium and a good source of vitamin A, B-complex, C and E.

Organic food for children

Going organic is an essential move for any adult who cares about health and the environment. Many consumers still consider it a luxury, given the price of organic food and the lifestyle considerations. However, children are a different matter altogether and the health implications of choosing anything other than organic for children can be very serious in the long term. Only now are we becoming aware of the problems associated with the modern diet and while there are undoubtedly serious short-term effects (see below), the long-term prospects of our chemical environment may be nothing short of disastrous.

From the very first moments of conception through to adulthood, children are growing and developing. Everything that goes into or onto their bodies will play a part in their overall health, both now and in the future. Because they are smaller, and their systems are less mature, children are more susceptible to chemicals than adults. They have a greater need for nutrients,

to ensure normal development and health, and they need to build up strong immunity to cope with the ever-increasing number of superbugs, viruses and potential allergens.

It is no coincidence that an increased number of miscarriages, stillbirths, childhood cancers, birth defects, heart disease, allergies and auto-immune conditions in children has coincided with the expansion of the processed, convenience food market, based on intensively farmed foods. Children need good, nutritious, fresh, healthy food and they need an environment that is as free from chemicals as possible. From the moment a parent makes a decision to have a baby, the emphasis has to be on reducing the load of toxins in food and in the products used in the home. The best and safest way to do this is to go organic.

Why organic?

- Preconception and pregnancy: There are now literally hundreds of studies showing a link between maternal eating habits and environmental factors, such as smoking, on the health of an unborn child. What they boil down to is the fact that a lack of key nutrients and a preponderance of toxins can have an effect on everything from birthweight, IQ, immunity, future fertility and susceptibility to allergies, to cancers, hyperactivity, sleep disorders and normal growth patterns. Choosing organic means ensuring a good intake of key nutrients while reducing exposure to harmful toxins.
- GM foods (see page 39): Organic foods contain no GMOs (genetically modified organisms), which could cause allergies, antibiotic resistance and possibly even genetic damage.
- Toxins: Organic foods and other products are free from toxic chemicals, which can have a serious impact on health. Organic food does not contain any of the thousands of artificial additives and preservatives, flavourings, colourings and sweeteners. All of these chemicals have an effect on immunity and digestion, and have been implicated in allergies.
- Food poisoning: Conventionally-produced food is rife with food-borne illnesses such as salmonella. Children are particularly susceptible to these types of infection, which can be a trigger for serious allergies and intolerance.
- Good eating habits: When children become accustomed to eating nutritious organic food – as opposed to conventional junk – good eating habits are established, which will help to keep them healthy in the present, while protecting their future.
- Immunity: Your child's immunity is his or her first and last defence against disease. Going organic, by eating organic food and choosing organic products, will help to build up a strong immune system, which is essential for life.

Organic for health

Children today eat a fairly unvaried diet, based around processed, 'kid-friendly' food. Not only are these foods high in chemicals that are known to cause health problems, but they provide very little in the form of nutrition. However, what you may not know is that even children eating a good diet, based on conventionally-farmed wholefoods and fresh fruits and vegetables may be heading for trouble. Governments around the world set safe limits for pesticides and other toxic chemicals used on foods today, but these levels are *not* altered for children. In other words, what may be an acceptable level for a fully grown man, will certainly not be safe for children.

All of the problems associated with conventionally grown food detailed in this book are relevant to children. In fact, their impact is intensified because children's bodies are smaller, their systems are less mature, their organs are less developed and they tend to eat much the same types of foods, which means that their intake of one or a group of pesticides can be much higher than average. For example, the average child tends to eat plenty of apples (whole or in apple juice), bananas, oranges and pears, all of which are heavily sprayed. Another popular choice is sweetcorn, which is now genetically modified. And children are the biggest drinkers of milk – a product that can contain numerous nasty things such as BST (a growth hormone used to increase milk production), antibiotics and GMOs.

And there's more. Conventionally farmed foods use many chemicals that can interfere with normal body functioning. Take the so-called gender-bender chemicals, for example. Some, including organochlorines (over 11,000 different organochlorines are used today, in products ranging from pesticides and plastics, through to dental fillings, toothpaste and mouthwash), can mimic the effect of natural substances such as oestrogen that play a key role in our reproductive systems. These hormone disrupters are believed to be responsible for birth defects, falling sperm counts, infertility and other reproductive problems such as early puberty and menopause – as well as decreasing our resistance to disease by suppressing our immune systems.

Furthermore, the number and level of antibiotics found in conventionally farmed animals is frightening. Consuming even low levels of antibiotics over a period of time can interfere with a child's immune system, making them more susceptible to colds and other infections, as well as allergies.

Organic food is a health essential for children. It provides them with the nutrients they need without the risks of conventionally farmed foods. Furthermore, it encourages a healthy, varied diet. If you take 'going organic' one step further, to ensure that your home environment is as organic and natural as possible, you'll be reducing the demands placed on your child's body. This allows the body to devote energy to growing, developing and becoming strong and healthy, rather than coping with the negative effects of chemicals.

What your child eats really matters. If you choose organic food, you are protecting your child from thousands of artificial additives that can cause health problems. You'll be ensuring that their diet is free of hormones that can affect their health on all levels, there will be no

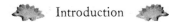

GMOs to worry about and many organic foods are sugar and salt free, or contain less of these ingredients than other brands. They don't contain hydrogenated oils or fats, which are now linked with cancer. What's more, children seem to be much less likely to show symptoms of allergy and intolerance when eating an organic food to which they were previously sensitive. Pesticides could well be at the root of this, but chances are that it is simply the cocktail of toxins that appear in the average meal that triggers problems.

How much needs to be organic?

The answer is as much as you can afford, based on the types of foods that your child eats most of. Organic formula is not that much more expensive than conventional brands and it is an important choice to make if you choose to bottle feed, largely because of the problems associated with the milk industry – and cows in general.

From there, it is not expensive to choose organic for first foods. For the first few months of weaning, babies use food to develop new tastes rather than for their nutritional value. However, if it sounds like a contradiction to use organic at this stage, it's not. Remember the damaging chemicals found in conventionally farmed foods.

Tips for going organic

- If your budget is tight, stick with the foods that your child eats the most of as he or she gets older. What you want to avoid is a preponderance of the same types of chemicals appearing over and over again. So if he is a big toast eater, choose organic bread. If he loves apple juice, buy organic.
- Similarly, most children seem to drink a great deal of milk, so it's sensible to reduce the risks by buying organic. Organic milk is not substantially more expensive and, once again, given the risks, all children should drink organic milk, particularly if they are also fond of cheese and yogurt too.
- Meat, eggs and root vegetables are most likely to contain dangerous chemicals that are the result of intensive farming. Children are most at risk of chemical residues and it is wise to play safe with these foods in particular. Remember that children do not need a lot of meat and can get protein from other sources.
- Grains are now particularly in the spotlight because they are so heavily sprayed and because the small grains absorb much more of these dangerous chemicals than some other foods. Given that most children eat toast, cereal, pasta and sandwiches regularly, it is sensible to buy organic. Once again, these are not significantly more expensive.
- Soya products should be organic, if possible. With the problems associated with genetic modification, it is sensible to buy something that you know does not contain GM ingredients.

- Buy as much organic produce as you can afford. If you eat too many fresh products to buy all organic, then wash everything very carefully and, in the extreme, peel it. There are now special detergents that remove waxes, pesticides and any other substances sprayed on the skin of fruits and vegetables, which can help to limit the damage.
- Organic food need not add much to your shopping bill. If you use it as a supplement to your ordinary shopping, you may notice a difference. However, by cutting out all the convenience and junk food, and focusing on a little meat, plenty of fruits and vegetables, some good pastas and breads, rice, pulses and dairy it can be much cheaper than a trolley-load of supermarket convenience foods.
- If your child is a canned-food junkie, it is definitely worth buying the organic options. Foods such as baked beans and soups can contain a wide variety of nasty ingredients and what should be nutritious may be nothing more than a can of chemicals. The organic options are much safer.
- Consider buying organic produce from a local greengrocer. They tend to be cheaper and the food is fresher, because it is generally collected from the market that same day. Another good option is an organic delivery service, which can be cheaper than supermarkets and very convenient.
- Choose organic fruits and vegetables that are in season. They are always much cheaper than imported goods.
- Use your freezer. If organic beans are on special offer in the supermarket, buy lots and freeze them.

Allergies and GM foods

Allergies are often caused by the protein elements in foods, and genetic engineering results in new proteins in food products. Gene foods could trigger allergic reactions (some serious enough to cause death), or they could encourage susceptibility to more allergens. The answer is to choose organic wherever possible, as it is the only real way to guarantee that a food or food product is free of GM ingredients.

Using this book

If you haven't already pinpointed your child's allergies or intolerances, you can do so by using some of the methods discussed earlier, including keeping a food diary and undertaking a gentle elimination programme. The recipes in this book are designed for children who suffer from the main allergies, although not all recipes are free of every potentially allergenic ingredient.

There are recipes for the weaning stages straight through to birthday party fun. Treats are not always healthy, but they are important to ensure that your child feels like his or her friends and able to indulge from time to time. Try to experiment with as many of the recipes as you can. Your child's repertoire of likes will increase and you can ensure that he doesn't develop poor eating habits that may lead to overeating certain foods. Moreover, you'll ensure that he is getting the nutrients he needs to become strong and healthy, and able to overcome allergies and intolerance naturally.

Every member of the family will benefit from the recipes in this book. Too often we depend upon the same foods, thereby setting the stage for sensitivities. Most of us, for example, eat far too much wheat and dairy produce. By making subtle changes – adding different grains, opting for non-dairy produce, eating fewer eggs, and using different forms of proteins – you'll ensure that your diet is varied enough to provide a foundation for good health on all levels.

Enjoy

Take pleasure in this book and take the time to experiment with different combinations of recipes. Try to ensure that your child's diet is as healthy and varied as possible, but always make sure that treats are available. You want to send the message that food is there to be enjoyed – that it need not be something to be feared. Most importantly, however, get your children involved in the cooking, let them help choose the menu, and experiment with variations and different combinations of food. Teach them how to choose the foods that make them feel good and will keep them strong and healthy. A little education goes a long way and, with the help of this book, you can help them to live normal lives, eating the same types of foods that their friends enjoy. Happy eating.

KAREN SULLIVAN

Introduction
to the recipes

I have always loved cooking: I love watching friends and family tucking into my food with glee and I love trying to find ways round the problems of creating delicious food without using certain ingredients.

In my books I have tried to share this love and knowledge of food so that adults and families can revel once again in the joy of cooking and eating together. Now I hope to go one step further by presenting 80 new recipes specifically designed for children of all ages, so that they too will be able to look forward to their next meal, instead of feeling singled out for special treatment or dreading their 'different' lunch box.

The recipes in this book are designed to provide a wide spectrum of foods for children who suffer from food allergies and intolerances. I have tried to cater for as many allergies as possible, though by necessity these are the most common. A nutritionist has vetted all the recipes in this book, and you can be sure that they are suitable by looking at the symbol system that is used at the top of each recipe. Please ensure you check the symbols when choosing a recipe – it would be so annoying to have done the shopping only to discover on closer inspection that the recipe is unsuitable.

I have included many recipes that are egg free, yeast free or avoid vegetables that are part of the nightshade family of plants (these are a well-known cause of sensitivities). Most of the recipes are gluten free, so that cooking for coeliacs will be easier and more exciting. Virtually all the recipes are lactose free, but you can always substitute some goat or sheep products if your children can digest them, as they are tastier than the soya and rice products that I have used. Lastly, the majority of the recipes are nut free but due to the nutritious content of almonds and Brazil nuts they have been included in a few recipes.

I have made a conscious effort to introduce a wide variety of different foods and fresh foods in this book, so that you can start educating your child's taste buds at a young age. Children have no preconceived ideas about food so it is up to you to help them to enjoy the huge spectrum of foods available. This way, hopefully, children will be steered away from the slippery road of too much sugar, salt and saturated fat, which is making more and more children overweight or setting them up for a lifetime of ill health and lethargy.

The recipes include everything from baby starter foods, to finger foods for toddlers, variations on the sort of convenience foods all kids enjoy, and a host of party dishes. The baby foods are not just nutritional but avoid toxins, unwanted sugars or likely allergens and in addition will not cause any strain to a baby's delicate digestive system. The first four recipes are really watery, for the real first timers, while the follow-up baby foods have more texture, to get the baby used to different consistencies. For two to three year olds I have included the sort of popular foods that you may not be able to buy from the frozen and convenience foods sections in supermarkets. These are the sort of products normally coated in breadcrumbs or batter, like fish fingers or chicken nuggets. Also, the mini pots of fromage frais or yogurt that most parents give their children are not an option for those on a lactose-free diet, so I have provided a recipe for lactose-free mini yogurts filled with fruits.

The rest of the recipes will suit children of all ages. Shakes, for example, are delicious and quick and can be whizzed up in minutes by parents or kids. They are not only nutritious, but also colourful and fun enough to tempt picky eaters into drinking fruit rather than eating it!

We have had so many requests from parents to include plenty of treats for packed lunches for school that I have racked my brains and come up with some yummy ideas for them. I do know how difficult it is for a child who feels excluded at meal times because they cannot have all the delicious goodies that other children enjoy. I hope these recipes will balance the books so that, in turn, the other children will envy them.

The problem with high teas and children's birthday parties is really when kids want to bring their friends home. None of the other children want to eat boring or bland food and it is unfair to give them scrumptious morsels if the birthday child cannot enjoy the same food. With this in mind, I have provided a selection of recipes that will keep all the children – guests and hosts alike – happy and full. A similar problem often crops up at various celebrations throughout the year, so I have also included a selection of recipes for Halloween, Christmas and Easter. Getting children involved in the process of cooking is important and you'll find the children can help to make many of these recipes – which makes it more fun for them.

So many parents, on top of looking after their family, have to go out to work as well – they come home late and tired and children often seem to graze instead of enjoying a family meal. Luckily, most parents have the weekends free and can spend time cooking and being with their children. Of course, catering for a child or children with food intolerances or allergies can make life a little more difficult so I have tried to make life easier by keeping the recipes as simple as possible – giving you more time to have fun and to play with your children.

Having resisted for years the persuasive arguments in favour of organic foods, I have to say that I have finally been lured by the advantages of organic produce. Instead of buying lots of cheap food I now buy less but better quality, organic food – not only to avoid chemicals and preservatives but also for the stronger and sweeter flavours that I remember from childhood. The extra expense of organic produce is balanced out by excluding nibbles, salty or sweet, that are of course baddies and no good for my figure or children's teeth!

Eating should be a pleasure for everyone and using the recipes in this book will enable you to present such delicious food that no toddler, child, teenager or adult will realize that they are enjoying anything out of the ordinary. Children have to have enjoyable treats, just as parents do, and this book is full of them, so that everyone can have fun together.

Symbols used throughout this book

The following symbols are very important. They are your guide to what is in each recipe. You can use each recipe with complete confidence knowing that a professional nutritionist has checked each one.

GF = GLUTEN FREE (which is wheat free)

WF = WHEAT FREE (which is not gluten free)

DF = DAIRY FREE and LACTOSE FREE

EF = EGG FREE

NF = NUT FREE

YF = YEAST FREE (which does not contain fresh or dried yeast)
The recipes considered to be yeast free are those that do not contain baker's yeast, brewer's yeast or a derivative, either on their own or within an ingredient. These recipes are suitable for children with an intolerance or allergy to yeast. Children or teenagers suffering from candida, however, also need to avoid foods that contain moulds or other fungi, as well as sugars and alcohols that feed yeasts and fungi. The yeast-free recipes in the book are not suitable for a candida diet.

 VEGETARIAN (this is suitable for vegetarians but not vegans)
V

Any one, or all, of these symbols is printed at the top of each recipe. Please be sure that you are not allergic or intolerant to any other substances in the ingredients.

Important information

- Throughout the book, all solid and liquid ingredients are given in metric first, followed by American imperial and cup measurements. Please follow one set of measurements in each recipe, as they are not interchangeable. All the recipes have been tested using both measurements.
- Unless otherwise stated all tablespoon or teaspoon measurements are level. All eggs are assumed to be medium unless otherwise stated. Most recipes indicated as egg free have the fresh egg quantity and instructions as well.
- There is a wide range of gluten- or wheat-free flour available; my favourite and the one that I used in every recipe is a particularly good mix made by Wellfoods Ltd. It is not available in the shops yet but can be purchased by mail order (see page 192). However, there are many other good flours available on the market or you can produce your own blend. Don't use just one kind of flour but mix something like rice flour with potato flour or barley flour, depending on your dietary needs. Please take into account that each variety of flour will have different absorbency levels and recipes must therefore be adjusted accordingly. Sometimes you may have to add a little more liquid if the mixture seems too dry; if the mixture is too wet you may need to add a fraction more flour. If you keep using the same brand of flour, you will soon be able to judge this without a moments thought.
- Please note that an asterisk beside an ingredient indicates that the product *may* contain gluten or wheat. This means you need to check the label to ensure that the variety that you buy is gluten and wheat free. Other specific ingredients are clearly described as gluten or wheat free and these can be purchased at large supermarkets or superstores, health food shops or by mail order.
- Throughout the ingredients lists, I have stated organic wherever I have easily been able to find an organic brand. The remaining ingredients may be available in an organic range but I have not stated this, as it would be annoying for you if you could not find such a product. I leave the final choice to you as to whether or not you buy organic foods.
- Yeast free as indicated in the symbols on page 44 is relevant to children with a severe yeast intolerance or allergy. There are recipes in the book that specifically avoid using fresh or dried yeast, for instance all the soda bread recipes. However, recipes may contain cheese or other ingredients that have moulds, fungi, sugars or alcohols, and these may not be suitable for a teenager on a candida diet.
- Salt should not be given to very young children and is therefore not included in any of the early recipes. The addition of salt is only actually necessary in a minority of recipes. Obviously, to most palates, food tastes better with salt but this is mostly because we become used to the taste. Over consumption of salt is undoubtedly a big health problem and as we do not need to add salt to our food (we obtain any salt we need from natural unadulterated foods), you may want to educate your child's palate *not* to become used to this taste. To remind you that you do have a choice, salt is listed as 'optional' in recipes where its use is

not essential. There are a few recipes where salt is obligatory (certain breads etc.) – in such cases the word 'optional' is omitted.

- A number of the recipes that do not appear in the vegetarian chapter can be adapted to suit vegetarians – so check all recipes to see if the vegetarian symbol is present.
- Please ensure that all hot dishes and ingredients are handled with care and that all food is served at a safe temperature for your babies and children.

Using egg replacers

I have used Orgran egg replacer in most of the recipes because I found that it was by far the best. In a few recipes I have given instructions on how to use some of the egg combinations given below, as they really do work very well. In most recipes, I have also included the number of fresh eggs needed so that anyone without an egg allergy can easily use the recipes. Good brands of egg replacers are available in well stocked health food stores and 'well-being' sections of superstores, as well as by mail order (see page 192 for suppliers).

Here are some suggestions for cheaper – though less convenient – ways of replacing eggs.

- Eggs are a liquid and generally, if you omit them, you need to substitute an equal amount of liquid. The yolks add softness and the whites add air bubbles. You can substitute some organic oil for the yolks and some shortening for the whites, plus some other liquid to make up the remainder of the total liquid measurement. For example, 2 eggs equals about 125ml/½ cup of liquid, therefore use (as an example), 2 tablespoons of oil, 2 tablespoons of shortening and 60ml/¼ cup of fruit purée.
- Many vegan books suggest using ground flax seeds, which results in baked goods that rise well and have a good texture. However, this method is only suitable for strong-tasting baked goods and not for a delicate sponge. To replace 1 egg, mix 1 tablespoon of ground flax seeds with 3 tablespoons of water and leave to settle for a few minutes before using as you would a whole egg.
- Another way of replacing an egg in a recipe is to mix the following ingredients:

  2 tablespoons gluten-free flour
  1½ teaspoons corn oil
  1 teaspoon gluten-free baking powder
  2 tablespoons water

Combine all the ingredients and use the mixture immediately as it loses its effectiveness within 2 hours.

- Other alternatives that you can experiment with are as follows (all replace 1 egg):

>   55g/2oz soft tofu blended with some water
>
>   ½ a mashed ripe banana
>
>   60ml/¼ cup applesauce or puréed fruit such as apricots (good in cookies)
>
>   1 tablespoon soya flour mixed with 1 tablespoon water
>
>   1 teaspoon yeast dissolved in 60ml/¼ cup warm water
>
>   1½ tablespoons water mixed with 1½ tablespoons oil and 1 heaped teaspoon gluten- and wheat-free baking powder
>
>   1 tablespoon arrowroot powder mixed with 3 tablespoons water
>
>   1 tablespoon pure cornflour (cornstarch) mixed with 3 tablespoons water
>
>   ¼ teaspoon of Xanthan gum mixed with 60ml/¼ cup water, let it stand until it thickens – it can then be whipped like an egg white (use it to replace 1–2 eggs)

Play around with these mixtures to discover which ones suit different recipes and, more importantly, the taste buds of your children.

My Store Cupboard

This is a list of some of the basic foods I keep in my store cupboard. Obviously it does not cater for every type of food allergy or intolerance, but it may provide some useful ideas.

> ANTOINETTE SAVILL SIGNATURE SERIES GLUTEN-FREE WHITE LOAF
>
> ORGANIC ALLERGY-FREE CORN FLAKES AND RICE POPS OR KRISPIES
>
> ORGANIC UNSULPHURED DRIED FRUITS, SULTANAS AND RAISINS
>
> ORGANIC ALMONDS, BRAZIL NUTS AND PINE NUTS
>
> EXTRA VIRGIN FIRST COLD PRESSED OLIVE OIL, FLAX SEED OIL AND ORGANIC SUNFLOWER OIL
>
> SEL DE GUÉRANDE SEA SALT
>
> PURE VANILLA EXTRACT
>
> BOYAJIAN PURE CITRUS OILS (LIME, LEMON AND ORANGE) FOR ICING AND CAKES
>
> ORGANIC RICE, MILLET AND RYE FLAKES AND PORRIDGE OATS FOR MUESLI
>
> PURE ORGANIC HONEY, MAPLE SYRUP AND ORGANIC BLACKSTRAP MOLASSES
>
> WELLFOODS GLUTEN-FREE FLOUR MIX, OAT FLOUR, RICE FLOUR, BARLEY FLOUR AND BUCKWHEAT FLOUR
>
> TOMOR KOSHER, OTHER DAIRY-FREE MARGARINE AND ORGANIC DAIRY-FREE SOFT MARGARINE (PURE)
>
> ORGANIC CANNED BUTTER (LIMA) BEANS, CHICKPEAS (GARBANZOS) AND SWEETCORN KERNELS

GLUTEN-FREE INSTANT OR FAST-ACTION YEAST

PURE CORNFLOUR (CORNSTARCH)

HEINZ UK (CHECK LABEL) BAKED BEANS WITHOUT SUGAR

GELATINE OR VEGETARIAN EQUIVALENT

ORGANIC SESAME, PUMPKIN, POPPY AND SUNFLOWER SEEDS

GLUTEN-FREE SPICE MIXTURES AND GROUND CINNAMON

GLUTEN-FREE BAKING POWDER, CREAM OF TARTAR AND BICARBONATE OF SODA (BAKING SODA)

ORGANIC CIDER VINEGAR

ORGANIC BROWN RICE AND BARLEY

ORGRAN GLUTEN- AND YEAST-FREE PASTA, ALPHABET SHAPES AND ORGANIC PRODUCTS

ORGANIC TOMATO PURÉE (PASTE) AND PASSATA (ITALIAN SIEVED TOMATOES)

PROVAMEL SOYA ORGANIC UNSWEETENED PLAIN AND SOME FLAVOURED MILKS

ALMOND MILK AND BIO RICE MILK

ORGANIC READY-MADE POLENTA

ORGRAN NO EGG NATURAL EGG REPLACER

CAROB POWDER, FLAKES, DROPS OR BARS

DAIRY-FREE CHOCOLATE BARS OR DROPS

In the deep-freeze

ANTOINETTE SAVILL SIGNATURE SERIES WHITE BREAD ROLLS AND PIZZA BASES

TOFUTTI OR SWEDISH GLACÉ ICE CREAM DESSERTS

ORGANIC CHICKEN BREASTS AND DRUMSTICKS

ORGANIC FROZEN VEGETABLES

In the refrigerator

AT LEAST A HALF A DOZEN OF BOTH MEDIUM AND LARGE ORGANIC FREE-RANGE EGGS

PROVAMEL YOFU AND OTHER YOGURTS

REDWOOD WHOLEFOOD COMPANY CHEEZLY DAIRY-FREE FETA-STYLE CHEESE AND GRATED CHEDDAR-STYLE CHEESE

TOFUTTI MOZZARELLA-STYLE CHEESE SLICES, SOUR CREAM AND THEIR THREE FLAVOURS OF SOFT CREAM CHEESE

GRANOVITA MAYOLA EGG-FREE MAYONNAISE

Super quick hit list of danger foods

As you will have no doubt discovered, avoiding certain foods can be a tricky business. If you need to avoid wheat, for instance, it may be easy to avoid bread and cakes but what about all the other minor sources that you may not even have considered? The general introduction highlighted the various names given to foods that commonly cause sensitivity, as well as some of the sources. The following lists are simply a quick reminder of some of the ingredients and products to avoid or that require you to check the label.

Gluten-free diet
GF   Watch out for:

Rye, barley, durum wheat (pasta), semolina, sausages and pies, malt, malt vinegar, oats, wheat flour, bran, prepared stuffing and mixes, starch (including modified starch), rusk, mixed (pie) spice and other blends. All prepared chiller cabinet foods, sauces, canned and frozen foods. Some chocolates and American-style ice creams. All bakery goods.

Wheat-free (and gluten-free) diet
WF   Watch out for:

Wheat protein, binder, thickener or thickening, bread sticks, pita breads and wraps, Tortillas, Nachos chips with a mix of wheat and corn, Yorkshire puddings, noodles, cakes, cookies, pastries, scones and doughnuts, breads and pancakes. Some chocolates and American-style ice creams. All prepared chiller cabinet foods, sauces, canned and frozen foods.

Dairy-free diet
DF   Watch out for:

Butter, buttermilk, cheese, cream, yogurt, ice creams and frozen desserts, hydrolysed whey protein, lactose, lactic acid, casein, margarine or shortening containing whey, milk solids, non-milk fat solids, skimmed milk powder, whey, batter and cake mixes, hot chocolate mixes, condensed or evaporated milk, custards, mashed potato, cake toppings, rice pudding and instant mixes. All prepared chiller cabinet foods, sauces, canned and frozen foods. Chocolates and sweets.

Egg-free diet

EF Watch out for:

Albumen, dried egg, egg glaze, egg lecithin, egg white, egg yolk, meringues, batter mixes, batter or breadcrumb-coated food, bedtime drinks, beef burgers and meat balls, custard, ice creams and frozen desserts, quiche and pastries, mayonnaise and sauces, Scotch egg and pork pies, spaghetti and pasta. Cake, pastry and cookie mixes.

Nut-free diet

NF Watch out for:

Nut oils, nut butters, almond or other milks, chocolates and all confectionery. All goods from the bakery, vegetarian or vegan prepared or frozen foods or mixes, ice creams and frozen desserts, cake and cookie mixes, vegetable stock/bouillon powders, Christmas mincemeat, cakes and puddings, breakfast cereals and crisps (chips).

Yeast-free diet

YF Watch out for:

Alcoholic beverages, malted drinks and milk, ginger ales and root beer, frozen and canned citrus fruit and grape juices, all baked bread products, croûtons, pretzels, stuffing, baking mixes, malted cereals and baby foods, cereals containing added vitamins or dried fruit, ketchup, mayonnaise, mustard, soy sauce or pickles. Any dip, topping or sauce with vinegar in. Meat products using rusk such as sausages and hamburgers, pickled meats or vegetables, mushrooms, very ripe bruised vegetables or fruits.

ANTOINETTE SAVILL

Index of recipes

With the exception of the chapters on baby foods, the recipes in this book are categorized in accordance with normal cookbook practice; that is into soups, fish, vegetarian dishes, desserts and so on. The following list is designed to illustrate which recipes are suitable for particular age groups, meal situations and special occasions.

Starter baby foods

Pea and pear purée 56
Parsnip and squash purée 57
Avocado and broccoli purée 58
Spinach and cauliflower purée 59
Rusks 68

Follow-up baby foods

Pasta, sweetcorn and leek mash 62
Sweet potato, chickpea and parsley mash 63
Brown rice, apple and mango mash 64
Alphabet pasta with sweet tomato sauce 65
Barley risotto 66
Rusks 68

Finger foods for toddlers

Breadsticks 187
White bread 186
Rusks 68
Fishcakes and fish fingers 104
Yeast-free pizza 128
Polenta chips and tomato ketchup 98
Mini Scotch eggs 82
Mini quiches 85
Little fruit yogurt pots 142
Cherry muffins 169
Animal cookies 158
Airy fairy cakes 164
Blueberry pancakes with raspberry sauce 144

Tottering twos and three year olds

Sweet potato and coconut soup 76
Bean and leek soup 77
Creamy cheesy dip with salsa 84
Hummus dip with baked potato skins and crudités 80
Chicken and pesto pasta shapes 114
Chicken in organic crisps 116
Chicken nuggets and tomato ketchup 117
Chickpea and pasta salad 93
Corn and watercress fritters with sticky drumsticks 112
Toad in the hole 124
Gnocchi with sage and lemon sauce 88
Spaghetti Carbonara style 126
Baked hedgehog potatoes 91
Hot chocolate fudge magic pudding 154
Steamed blueberry pudding 150
Blueberry pancakes with raspberry sauce 144
Bramble fool 140
Castle puddings 148
Raspberry ripple ice cream 134
Chunky monkey chocolate ice cream 136
Mini chocolate muffins 166
Chocolate soda bread 182
Apple and raisin loaf 180

 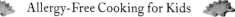

From Tots to Teens

Shakes
Papaya, apple and pineapple fruit shake 70
Chocolate and banana soya milk shake 71
Raspberry and vanilla rice shake 72

Breakfasts
Pick and mix muesli 185
Blueberry pancakes with raspberry sauce 144
Rye and oat soda bread 183
White bread 186
Bacon cheesy corn muffins 184

Packed lunches
Chickpea and pasta salad 93
Mini quiches 82
Mini Scotch eggs 85
Chicken tikka wraps 110
Chocolate soda bread 182
Carob chip and Brazil nut cookies 160
Apple and raisin loaf 180
Lemon and pine nut tarts 162
Cherry muffins 169

Kids' high teas
Tuscan salad 90
Macaroni cheese 92
Chicken in organic crisps 116
Chicken nuggets and tomato ketchup 117
Fishcakes and fish fingers 104
Polenta chips and tomato ketchup 98
Toad in the hole 124
Chicken and pesto pasta shapes 114
Baked hedgehog potatoes 91
Pile high pizza 96
Yeast-free pizza 128
Gnocchi with sage and lemon sauce 88
Super cheat's berry ice cream 137
Chocolate or carob fudge sauce 141

Family lunches and suppers
Bean and leek soup 77
Minestrone with cheesy toasts 74
Sweet potato and coconut soup 76
Chicken tikka wraps 110
Bashed-up chicken 115
Lamb moussaka 130
Barley risotto 66
Potato, cheese and parsley pie 94
Yeast-free pizza 128
Salmon penne with pine nuts 108
Fennel, corn and fish pie 106
Cheesy roulade 100
Corn and watercress fritters with sticky
    drumsticks 112
Spaghetti Carbonara style 126
Tuscan salad 90
Apple and almond butterscotch tart 146
Steamed blueberry pudding 150
Castle puddings 148
Upside down pineapple ginger pudding 152
Hot chocolate fudge magic pudding 154
Chilled vanilla cheesecake 138
Bramble fool 140
Chunky monkey chocolate ice cream 136
Raspberry ripple ice cream 134
Super cheat's berry ice cream 137
Chocolate or carob fudge sauce 141

Halloween party
Hummus dip with baked potato skins and
    crudités 80
Halloween chicken in a pumpkin 118
Carob apples on sticks 161
Airy fairy cakes 164
Chocolate or carob fudge sauce 141

 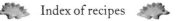

Christmas parties
Leftover turkey and noodle soup 78
Roast turkey with salad leaf and potato
    stuffing 120
Mini mince pies 170
Yule log 172
Christmas cake 174

Easter parties
Easter chocolate nest 176
Chocolate football birthday cake 178
Airy fairy cakes 164
Chocolate soda bread 182
Chocolate or carob fudge sauce 141

Birthday tea parties
Mini quiches 82
Mini Scotch eggs 85
Pile high pizza 96
Yeast-free pizza 128
Chicken in organic crisps 116
Chicken nuggets and tomato ketchup 117
Raspberry ripple ice cream 134
Chocolate football birthday cake 178
Airy fairy cakes 164
Carob apples on sticks 161
Chocolate soda bread 182
Sugar-free almond brownies 168
Mini chocolate muffins 166
Animal cookies 158

Starter baby foods

Pea and Pear Purée

Introducing solid foods to a baby should be fun – it's so exciting to watch them experiencing new tastes and textures. If your baby doesn't like a certain mixture then don't persist with it, try some other combination. Babies have preferences too!

   Most vegetable mixtures freeze but this mixture doesn't (nor do potato-based purées).

Makes 125ml/½ cup

GF	WF	DF	EF	NF	YF	V

125g/1 cup organic frozen peas
80ml/⅓ cup filtered water
½ small very ripe and sweet organic pear, peeled, core removed and roughly chopped

Steam the peas until tender or boil them in the filtered water until cooked through. Drain and allow them to cool. Blend the peas in a food processor with the pear.

Parsnip and Squash Purée

There are hundreds of purée combinations that you can make in bulk and freeze as first foods. Freeze them in ice cube trays, then wrap individually, seal and keep frozen until needed. You can experiment with your baby's taste buds by mixing different batches of frozen purée together to create new tastes and textures.

Butternut squash is easily digested and, like other orange fruits and vegetables, it is rich in beta-carotene.

Makes 500ml/2 cups

GF WF DF EF NF YF V

255g/9oz organic butternut squash, peeled, pith and seeds discarded and flesh roughly chopped
255g/9oz organic parsnip, peeled and roughly chopped
80ml/⅓ cup filtered water

Steam the squash and parsnips together for 8–10 minutes until soft. Allow to cool then purée with the water in a blender or food processor. Serve or freeze the portions in ice cube trays until needed.

Avocado and Broccoli Purée

Raw food purées are ideal for serving to your baby as they are a good source of vitamins, minerals, water and fibre. Avocado has plenty of essential oils and vitamin E, while broccoli is rich in beta-carotene and vitamin C.

This recipe doesn't freeze but it is an ideal way of using up a bit of avocado left over from lunch. Avocado turns brown and doesn't keep, so make and serve the purée straight away.

Makes 125ml/½ cup

100g/3½oz organic broccoli florets, cut into small pieces
80ml/⅓ cup filtered water
1 heaped tablespoon soft organic avocado flesh

Wash the broccoli carefully and then steam until tender or boil in the filtered water. Drain and cool the broccoli then blend in a food processor with the avocado and enough water to reach the desired consistency.

Spinach and Cauliflower Purée

Here is another bright, cheerful-looking purée for starting a baby on the voyage of food taste and texture discovery. This recipe makes quite a few servings and can be frozen for later use.

Makes 500ml/2 cups

GF   WF   DF   EF   NF   YF   V

200g/7oz organic frozen spinach leaves
125g/1 cup organic frozen cauliflower florets, cut into small pieces
80ml/⅓ cup filtered water

Cook the spinach and cauliflower together in a pan with the filtered water until the cauliflower is just tender. Drain the vegetables over a bowl so that you can use the cooking liquid, which contains vitamins and minerals.

Purée the vegetables with a little of the cooking liquid at a time in a blender or food processor. Freeze what you don't use in ice cube trays.

Follow-up baby foods

Pasta, Sweetcorn and Leek Mash

Carbohydrates provide energy and are therefore literally fuel for humans. Complex carbohydrates – which are unrefined, sustaining and contain vitamins, minerals and other key nutrients – are vital for overall nutrition, so here is something packed with goodness for your baby.

Makes enough for about 12 ice cubes

30g/½ cup gluten-free pasta shapes (check label for other allergens)
80g/½ cup organic sweetcorn kernels, drained if canned (without salt or sugar) or cooked until tender if frozen or fresh and drained
125g/½ cup finely sliced small organic leek
60ml/¼ cup filtered water

Cook the pasta shapes according to the instructions on the packet, drain, refresh with some filtered water, transfer to a food processor and add the prepared sweetcorn.

Meanwhile, cook the leeks in enough boiling filtered water to cover until they are soft. Drain the leeks. Add the leeks to the pasta mixture with the 60ml/¼ cup of water and process briefly. The consistency should be that of a coarse mash.

Freeze what you don't use in ice cube trays.

Sweet Potato, Chickpea and Parsley Mash

Proteins come from vegetable products as well as meat and other animal products, and the chickpeas (garbanzos) and sweet potatoes in this recipe are a valuable source of healthy protein. The parsley has plenty of calcium for growing teeth and bones.

GF WF DF EF NF YF V

Makes about 500ml/2 cups

1 large organic sweet potato, peeled, chopped and steamed until soft
2 heaped tablespoons drained, canned organic chickpeas (garbanzos), cooked without salt or sugar
100ml/scant ½ cup filtered water
1 tablespoon chopped fresh parsley

Put the cooked potato into a food processor, blend briefly until it become a lumpy mash and then add the chickpeas (garbanzos) and water. Process until a coarse mash is achieved and stir in the parsley. Reheat as much as you need and freeze the remainder in ice cube trays.

Brown Rice, Apple and Mango Mash

Brown rice is an excellent source of fibre, while the fruit contains plenty of vitamins. Use very ripe mango and apple so that the dish is sweet.

Makes 500ml/2 cups

GF   WF   DF   EF   NF   YF   V

55g/⅓ cup steamed organic brown rice, cold

1 small sweet organic eating apple, peeled, cored and stewed in a little filtered water

¼ of a small sweet ripe organic mango, peeled and roughly chopped

80ml/⅓ cup filtered water

Put all the ingredients into a food processor and blend until the mixture reaches a coarse, mashed consistency not a purée. Heat through the amount you need and keep the remainder chilled in the refrigerator for the next day.

Alphabet Pasta with Sweet Tomato Sauce

Tiny alphabet pasta is ideal for 9–12-month-old babies. The tomato sauce is sweetened with carrots, which makes it more appealing for babies. You could make double or treble the amount of sauce and freeze it in suitable amounts for instant food on extra busy days.

OPTIONAL

GF   WF   EF   NF   V   DF   YF

Makes about 6 portions

130g/4½oz organic carrots, scraped clean and finely chopped

400g/14oz organic tomatoes, skinned, seeded and chopped or use canned organic variety

30g/1oz dairy-free margarine (use organic butter if not following a dairy-free diet)

70g/2½oz dairy-free grated hard cheese or yeast-free cheese (see page 192 for brands and stockists) or use Pecorino sheep's cheese if not on a dairy-free diet

3 heaped tablespoons gluten-free alphabet vegetable rice pasta (I use Orgran, which comes in a 200g/7oz packet) – check label for other allergens

---

Bring a small pan of water to the boil, add the carrots and cook until tender. Meanwhile, cook the tomatoes in a small pan with the margarine or butter until soft and mushy. Remove the pan of tomatoes from the heat and stir in the cheese. Remove the carrots from the pan using a slotted spoon and cook the pasta in the carrot water until al dente (check timings on the back of the packet).

Meanwhile, place the carrots and the tomato mixture in a food processor and purée until smooth. Drain the pasta, combine with the sauce and serve warm. Cool and freeze the remainder in suitable-sized portions.

Barley Risotto

You can make this risotto for babies from about 10–12 months but make sure the turkey and vegetables are cut up very small, make it without seasoning or cheese and serve it tepid. This recipe is for the whole family, so serve the remainder hot, well seasoned and with plenty of cheese.

Barley isn't used nearly enough in our diets, which is a great shame because it is nutritious, versatile, filling and warming. Use it in place of white rice and you will create delicious soups, salads or risottos. Pot barley contains protein, vitamin B, calcium and iron, as well as plenty of fibre. Pearl barley is better for children under the age of about nine months as it has had its bran and germ removed and is therefore easier to swallow and digest. You can make up your own risottos according to your child's dietary needs – for example, add flaked salmon or tuna, organic leafy green vegetables, parsley, chicken, garlic, legumes and carrots to hike up the calcium and B vitamins.

OPTIONAL

Makes about 4–6 family portions plus baby or freeze in baby portions

GF   WF   DF   EF   NF   YF   V

340g/12oz organic pot barley, soaked in filtered cold water overnight

55g/2oz dairy-free margarine plus 1 heaped teaspoon

225g/8oz organic turkey fillet (omit for vegetarian), chopped into bite-size pieces

2 organic spring onions (salad onions), heavily trimmed and thinly sliced

2 organic carrots, peeled and finely chopped

Optional for older kids – ½ an organic garlic clove, peeled and crushed

55g/2oz organic French beans or fine green beans, trimmed and cut into short lengths

100g/3½oz organic broccoli florets (peas, broad beans, sweetcorn are also good), cut into small pieces

425g/15oz can chicken broth/bouillon (check label for allergens) and the same again of cold filtered water
   (use allergy-free vegetable stock for vegetarians)

Sea salt and freshly ground black pepper (optional according to age group)

100g/3½oz organic Savoy cabbage or spinach leaves, very finely shredded

2 tablespoons chopped fresh parsley

Plenty of grated dairy-free Cheddar-style cheese (not for yeast-free diet) or Florentino Parmezano (which is
   yeast free) or grated Pecorino sheep's cheese if not on a dairy-free diet

---

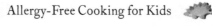 Allergy-Free Cooking for Kids

Drain the barley and rinse in cold filtered water. Melt the 55g/2oz of margarine in a non-stick pan, add the turkey, if using, onions and carrots and cook over medium heat for about 3 minutes, stirring from time to time. Stir in the garlic, if using, beans, broccoli and barley and cook for another 2 minutes.

Add the broth/bouillon, season lightly with salt and pepper, if using, and bring to the boil. Reduce the heat slightly and cook the barley at bubbling point until tender – this may take about 30 minutes. Stir the risotto from time to time, adding the water and more if necessary. Add the cabbage about 5 minutes before the risotto is ready.

At the last minute, stir in the heaped teaspoon of margarine, the parsley and about half the grated cheese. Serve straight away, sprinkled with the remaining cheese.

Rusks

Rusks are wonderful for babies to chew on but are inevitably made of wheat products. This recipe shows you how to make your own using the bread recipe on page 186. Make as many as you need for a couple of days.

Use part of a large white loaf made using the recipe on page 186, which uses Wellfoods gluten-free white flour but has yeast and egg in the recipe, or

A ready-made gluten-free white loaf with yeast and egg (see page 192 for brand and stockists), or

Use a white loaf made from a ready-to-make gluten-free white loaf mix without yeast or egg such as Orgran (see page 192 for brand and stockists)

Preheat the oven to 150°C/300°F/Gas mark 2.

Cut the cold bread into thick slices. Remove the crusts and, using a large pastry or cookie cutter, cut out a circle from each slice. Place the bread circles on a non-stick baking tray and bake in the oven for about 1 hour until they are nice and hard.

Use the offcuts of bread for making breadcrumbs – great for Queen of Puddings or bread sauce.

Shakes

Papaya, Apple and Pineapple Fruit Shake

This is really just liquid fruit salad but it is quicker to make and fun for older children if served in cool tall glasses with trendy straws. The fruit is packed with vitamins, minerals and fibre, so this is an excellent replacement for the unhealthy sugar- and salt-laden snacks that kids are often offered.

Makes about 1 serving

A little crushed ice, made with filtered water

¼ of a ripe organic papaya, peeled and roughly chopped

55g/2oz organic eating apple, roughly chopped (skin on but the core and pips removed)

A small piece of organic root ginger, grated (no need to peel)

1 slice of peeled, cored ripe organic pineapple, roughly chopped

80ml/⅓ cup filtered water

Put all the ingredients into a blender and process until smooth. Serve immediately with a little extra crushed ice and the kids have a super cool chiller for the summer.

Chocolate and Banana Soya Milk Shake

My little nieces, Lara and Ella, love milk shakes. This recipe is simple, nutritious and sweet, and an ideal snack for any child. If soya products cannot be tolerated but gluten or nut products can, you can use oat (Organic Oatly) or almond milk mixed with organic dairy-free cocoa powder and a little maple syrup to balance the cocoa. If this isn't appropriate, use rice milk instead.

Makes about 2 servings

250ml/1 cup chocolate flavoured soya milk (Provamel)
½ a small or ¼ of a large ripe organic banana, peeled

Empty the flavoured milk into a blender and slice the banana into it. Seal and blend until smooth. Serve immediately.

Raspberry and Vanilla Rice Shake

This is a soya-free shake that you can make with any soft fruit in season. Providing your kids are not gluten or nut intolerant you could substitute either oat (Organic Oatly) or almond milk for the rice milk – both are also delicious in this recipe.

Makes 1–2 servings

250ml/1 cup vanilla rice milk
55g/2oz fresh ripe organic raspberries
A few drops of pure vanilla extract

Place all the ingredients in a blender and process until smooth. Sieve the mixture, pour the shake into a glass or tumbler and add a bit of pizzazz with a technicoloured straw.

Soups, starters and snacks

Minestrone with Cheesy Toasts

This filling dish is really just a vegetable broth with cheese on toast on top. It is typical of the Italians to create something delicious yet cheap from everyday ingredients – in this case cabbage leaves and pasta.

Makes about 6 servings

255g/9oz organic dried cannellini beans, soaked overnight or 2 x 300g/10½oz cans cannellini beans

250ml/1 cup allergy-free vegetable bouillon/stock*

2 organic celery sticks, trimmed and any tough strings pulled off and discarded

3 tablespoons cold pressed extra virgin olive oil

1 organic onion, roughly chopped

2 organic carrots, thickly sliced into rings

2 organic potatoes, peeled and roughly chopped

1–2 organic garlic cloves, crushed

4 heaped tablespoons organic passata (Italian sieved tomatoes)

255g/9oz organic Savoy cabbage, trimmed and finely shredded

1.25 litres/5 cups water

1 tablespoon chopped fresh rosemary

1 tablespoon fresh thyme leaves

A pinch of sea salt (optional) and freshly ground black pepper

4 slices gluten-free white bread, crusts removed (see brand and stockists page 192) or a yeast- and egg-free bread

150g/5½oz packet grated dairy-free Cheddar-style hard cheese (see brand and stockists page 192) or use sheep's/goat's cheese if tolerated

55g/2oz soft organic dairy-free margarine (Pure is good)

or use dairy-free Mozzarella-style cheese slices (these are yeast free – see page 192 for brand and stockists)

* coeliacs please use gluten-free ingredients

Drain the beans and rinse under cold running water. Place them in a large pan, cover with fresh cold water and bring to the boil. Boil rapidly for 10 minutes, then lower the heat slightly and let them bubble away for about 1 hour or until the beans are tender, skimming off the scum and topping up the water level as necessary. If using canned beans, drain and rinse them and follow the remainder of the recipe.

Transfer about half of the beans to a food processor or blender and whiz with the bouillon/stock until smooth. Roughly chop the celery. Heat the oil in a large saucepan, add all the vegetables, except the cabbage, and cook gently, stirring frequently, for about 10 minutes until softened. Add the garlic, passata and puréed beans and stir well to mix. Now add the cabbage, water, rosemary, thyme and salt, if using, and pepper to taste. Stir in the remaining beans and bring to the boil, then cover and simmer at bubbling point for 30 minutes. Let the soup cool to a safe temperature.

At the last minute, toast the slices of bread on one side and then cover the uncooked side with the Cheddar-style cheese or goat's/sheep's cheese, dot with small blobs of margarine and grill (broil) until bubbling. If using mozzarella-style cheese, there's no need to dot with margarine, simply top the bread with the cheese and grill (broil). Cut each cheese on toast into quarters. Adults will need a whole slice but children will probably only need two of the quarters.

Ladle out the soup into bowls, top with the cheesy toasts and serve immediately.

Sweet Potato and Coconut Soup

Unbelievably smooth and delicate, this soup should suit all ages and can be very mild or quite hot. Sweet potatoes can be eaten by anyone who cannot eat ordinary potatoes, as they do not come from the same family.

Makes about 6 servings

1 large organic onion, finely chopped

800g/4 large organic sweet potatoes, peeled and cut into chunks

2 tablespoons cold pressed extra virgin olive oil

1½ teaspoons ground cumin

1½ teaspoons ground coriander

1 teaspoon freshly grated organic root ginger

Optional – a sprinkling of dried chilli flakes if this suits the youngest palate

2 teaspoons allergy-free vegetable bouillon/stock powder

1 litre/4 cups filtered water

15g/½oz fresh coriander (cilantro), chopped

400ml/14oz can organic coconut milk

Finely grated rind and juice of 1 unwaxed organic lime

Optional – an extra handful of fresh coriander (cilantro) leaves, roughly chopped for serving

---

Gently cook the onions and potatoes in the oil over medium heat for about 5 minutes until they turn gold at the edges. Add the cumin, coriander, ginger and chilli, if using, and continue to cook for about 1 minute. Sprinkle the potatoes with the bouillon/stock powder, pour over the water and bring to the boil. Reduce the heat a little and allow the soup to simmer for about 45 minutes until the potatoes are very soft. Add the coriander (cilantro) leaves and leave the soup to cool. Transfer to a blender or food processor, add the coconut milk and blend until smooth.

Transfer the soup back to the saucepan, add the grated lime and juice and reheat. You can serve the soup plain to younger children and sprinkle the rest of the bowls of soup with the extra coriander (cilantro).

Bean and Leek Soup

This is such a filling soup for winter that we often just have a bowl of this and some warm homemade soda bread (see page 183) for lunch, followed by piles of fruit. The Bacon Cheesy Muffins (see page 184) are brilliant with the soup too.

Makes about 6 servings

250g/1½ cups organic butter beans (lima beans), soaked overnight in a bowl of cold water and then drained just before use

1 medium organic onion, finely chopped

2 tablespoons cold pressed extra virgin olive oil

3 thick rashers organic smoked, rindless back bacon, finely chopped

2 large organic leeks, trimmed of tough outer layers and roughly chopped

1 organic garlic clove

750ml/3 cups filtered water

750ml/3 cups allergy-free vegetable or chicken stock/bouillon

2 bay leaves

12 sage leaves

Sea salt (optional), freshly ground black pepper and grated nutmeg

Bring a pan of water to the boil and add the beans. Cook at bubbling point for about 1 hour and then drain and refresh the beans under cold running water. If using canned beans, drain and rinse under cold running water.

Heat the oil in a pan, add the onions and bacon and cook over medium heat until the bacon is golden but not browned. Add the leeks and garlic and cook for a few minutes, stirring from time to time. Add the beans and cover with the water and the stock/bouillon. Stir in the bay leaves, sage, and season with salt, if using, pepper and a little grated nutmeg.

Let the soup cook at bubbling point for about 40 minutes, then remove from the heat and allow to cool. Liquidize the cooled soup in batches, until smooth, and then transfer back to the pan to reheat.

Leftover Turkey and Noodle Soup

Good news – something different to create for hungry teenagers from leftover turkey! We had an organic turkey recently and I have to confess that the taste and texture were so wonderful the frozen supermarket brands bore no comparison. There was a unanimous family vote that it was worth every penny and the trip to the butcher.

Makes 4–8 servings

2 large cooked organic turkey wings

2 sticks lemon grass, tough layers removed and discarded

1 organic onion, sliced

2 organic carrots, peeled and quartered

1 organic leek, trimmed and quartered

3cm/1¼in organic root ginger, not peeled but sliced

3 tablespoons fish sauce*

1 teaspoon organic honey

1 tablespoon organic soy sauce*

1 tablespoon sesame oil or organic cold pressed sunflower oil

1–2 organic garlic cloves, peeled and crushed

Optional – 1 mild chilli, trimmed, seeds removed and sliced (according to age group)

2 teaspoons (or less according to age group) Schwartz Thai 7 spice powder* (check label for allergens)

1 tablespoon sesame seeds

1 bunch organic spring onions (salad onions), trimmed and thinly sliced

200g/¾ cup canned and drained bean sprouts (use fresh if available and increase quantity if you want to stretch the soup)

Sea salt (optional) and freshly ground black pepper

125g/1 cup chopped cooked organic turkey meat (increase as desired)

255g/9oz packet thin Thai stir-fry rice noodles* (instant/4 minute type)

Optional – handful of fresh coriander (cilantro) leaves, finely chopped

* coeliacs please use gluten-free ingredients

Make the broth/bouillon first. Put the turkey wings, one lemon grass stick, onion, carrots, leek, ginger, fish sauce and a little salt, if using, into a big pan. Bring to the boil and then reduce the heat and simmer at bubbling point for about 1 hour.

Strain the broth, discard the ingredients in the sieve and transfer the broth to a large, clean pan. Stir in the honey and soy sauce and adjust the seasoning with salt, if using, and pepper.

Meanwhile, cook the noodles according to the instructions on the packet. Drain them and rinse under cold running water.

Heat the oil in a wok and add the garlic and chilli, if using, the remaining lemon grass, Thai 7 spice powder, sesame seeds, spring onions (salad onions) and bean sprouts and stir-fry for a couple of minutes. Add the chopped turkey meat, noodles, coriander (cilantro) leaves, if using, and pour over the broth. Please check the temperature of the soup before giving it to children.

Hummus Dip with Baked Potato Skins and Crudités

This is a popular and healthy starter at any time of the year and is also brilliant for barbecues, hungry teenagers and vegetarians. With any luck, by mixing potato skins and crudités, the kids will eat some of both.

Serves about 12

GF WF DF EF NF V

500g/1lb 2oz gluten- and dairy-free frozen fried potato skins or make your own with about 12 medium organic potatoes

A pinch of sea salt (optional) and freshly ground black pepper

Cold pressed extra virgin olive oil for brushing

A selection of prepared, organic carrots batons, cauliflower florets, mini vine tomatoes, and slices of cucumber, fennel and red pepper

Hummus

620g/3½ cups canned organic chickpeas (garbanzos), drained

2 heaped tablespoons organic light tahini paste

Optional – 1 large organic garlic clove, peeled and chopped

Optional – a few drops of chilli sauce* or a tiny bit of fresh sliced chilli, seeds removed

Juice of 2 large organic unwaxed lemons

255g/9oz packet organic tofu

A pinch of sea salt (optional) and freshly ground black pepper

A little chopped fresh parsley for decoration

* coeliacs please use gluten-free ingredients

Preheat the oven to 200°C/400°F/Gas mark 6.

Place the frozen potato skins on a non-stick baking sheet, sprinkle with salt, if using, and pepper, brush with oil and bake in the preheated oven until crispy. Alternatively, make your own by cutting thick slices off each potato (use the remaining flesh for mashed potato or soup). Brush the skin and flesh with the oil and bake until crispy on each side and cooked through on the inside. You could also make chunky wedges, which are easier for younger children to hold.

Whilst the potato skins are baking, make the hummus. Mix the chickpeas (garbanzos), tahini, garlic, chilli sauce or fresh chilli, if using, lemon juice, tofu, salt, if using, and pepper together in the food processor until smooth. Loosen the mixture to the desired consistency with a little cold filtered water or more lemon juice, according to age group.

Scoop into a dish and sprinkle with parsley. Place in the centre of a large plate and arrange the warm crispy potato skins around one side of the dip and the crudités on the other side. Serve immediately.

Mini Quiches

These quiches really are tiny, so they are ideal for packed lunches, picnics or parties. It is a good way of coaxing children to eat tuna fish, salmon or vegetables because the cheese disguises them and they smell so tempting when freshly baked. If you want bigger ones, use normal muffins trays and make 12. As you will have more space in each tart, you can chop up the fillings less finely.

Makes 36

Pastry
125g/4½oz dairy-free margarine, cubed
255g/2 generous cups gluten-free flour mix
A pinch of sea salt (optional) and freshly ground black pepper
1 organic free-range egg, beaten
Some cold filtered water

Quiche mixture
250ml/1 cup soya cream
2 organic free-range eggs, beaten

Suggested fillings
• Approximately 70g/⅓ cup of drained and flaked tuna or cooked and flaked salmon fillet
• Approximately 6 rashers very finely chopped, cooked organic bacon
• Tiny pieces of cooked organic broccoli florets
• Finely chopped and cooked organic onions or leeks

Topping
A small amount of grated dairy-free hard cheese (see brand and stockists page 192) or yeast-free cheese or sheep's or goat's cheese if either can be tolerated

3 x 12-hole miniature non-stick bun or muffin trays and a 5cm/2in round fluted pastry cutter

Preheat the oven to 190°C/375°F/Gas mark 5.

Sieve the flour into a bowl with a pinch of salt, if using, and pepper. Rub the margarine into the flour. Add the beaten egg and enough water to make the ingredients come together into a ball. Knead gently until smooth. Roll out the pastry to a thickness of about 5mm/¼in and cut 36 rounds with a cookie cutter to line the tins.

In a bowl, combine the cream and eggs and season to taste with salt, if using, and pepper.

Sprinkle a tiny amount of your chosen filling into each pastry case and then fill up with the cream and egg mixture. Top each quiche with grated cheese and bake for about 15 minutes until set. Cool in the tins and eat warm or cold.

If you make 12 bigger quiches, extend the cooking time to about 25 minutes to ensure that the pastry is golden and the filling puffed up and set.

Creamy Cheesy Dip with Salsa

This quick and easy starter or dip is great for filling up hungry kids and has the added bonus of a heap of crunchy, healthy vegetables that look fun and colourful. If goat's cheese can be tolerated just use a mild goat's cream cheese mixed with some natural set goat's yogurt – you don't need to add any flavourings.

Serves about 8

GF WF DF EF NF V YF

---

2 × 225g/8oz tubs Tofutti dairy-free Creamy Smooth soft-cheese-style spread in either onion or garlic and herbs flavour (see page 192 for brands and stockists)

4 tablespoons soya cream

Sea salt (optional) and freshly ground black pepper

2 tablespoons roughly chopped basil, coriander (cilantro) or parsley

170g/6oz tub fresh ready-made gluten-free tomato salsa (not yeast free if it contains vinegar) or homemade, which is prepared with lemon juice for yeast free, but either way not bottled or canned as they are too runny

100g/generous ½ cup pimento-stuffed olives or pitted black olives* (in oil and not vinegar for yeast free)

1 small organic sweet red and 1 organic sweet yellow pepper, finely chopped

155g/5½oz packet gluten-, dairy- and nut-free corn chips

* coeliacs please use gluten-free ingredients

In a bowl, mix the cream-style cheese with the soya cream until smooth and of a dip-like texture. It must be firm enough to support the salsa and peppers on top. Season to taste with salt, if using, pepper and half the herbs. Spoon the mixture into a wide, shallow serving bowl and spread the salsa over the top.

Chop the olives in half and mix with the peppers and remaining herbs. Sprinkle the mixture all over the salsa. Serve the dip with the corn chips or cover and chill until needed but do eat on the day of making.

Mini Scotch Eggs

Quails eggs are the perfect size for this recipe. Mini Scotch eggs are ideal for parties, picnics or just as toddler finger food. You must source good quality gluten-free sausage meat or, if your child is intolerant to wheat rather than gluten, you can ask a butcher to make you up some rusk-free sausages.

GF or WF   DF   NF   YF

Makes 12

12 quails eggs
400g/14oz packet best quality gluten- or wheat-free organic pork sausages or sausage meat (check label for
    other allergens)
70g/½ cup organic sesame seeds
Extra virgin olive oil for frying

Cook the quail eggs for 3 minutes in boiling water. Drain and repeatedly cover with cold water until the eggs are cool enough to peel. Peel and set aside.

Slit each sausage skin with a sharp knife; peel the skin away from the meat and discard. Halve each sausage or take sections of sausage meat and flatten with the palm of your hands. Carefully wrap each portion around each egg and seal by pinching the meat together at the joining point. Sprinkle the sesame seeds onto a saucer and dip and roll the eggs until they are completely covered with seeds.

In a deep pan, heat enough oil to shallow fry the eggs. Add the eggs to the pan and, using two forks to turn them, make sure that they are golden all over and that the sausage meat is completely cooked through. Drain the eggs on absorbent kitchen paper and leave to cool.

Serve straight away, or pack them into picnic ware and keep refrigerated until needed.

Soups, starters and snacks

Polenta Toasties with Cheesy Ham

This recipe is easy, as ready-made blocks of polenta are now widely available – some health food stores also sell the organic version. You can of course add any topping that your children like, such as bacon and tomato or chicken and pesto. If you're serving this recipe to older kids, add a little black pepper or paprika to the cheese topping.

Makes 4

500g/1lb 2oz block organic ready-made polenta*
4 slices organic ham, trimmed of excess fat and cut into thick pieces
150g/5½oz packet grated dairy-free Cheezly Cheddar-style hard cheese (not yeast free) with a little dairy-free margarine or 4 Tofutti (yeast-free) mozzarella-style slices, halved
Optional – freshly ground black pepper or paprika

* coeliacs please use gluten-free ingredients

Slice the polenta into 8 thick slices. Grill (broil) the slices on each side until browned. Remove the polenta from the heat and quickly cover each one with overlapping pieces of ham. Spoon the grated cheese over the top and dot with small blobs of margarine. Lightly dust with pepper or paprika, if using, and grill (broil) until golden and bubbling. If using the mozzarella-style slices then place 1 half on each slice of polenta and ham and dust with pepper or paprika, is using. No margarine is needed. Grill (broil) as above.

Sandwich the slices together and serve.

Vegetarian dishes

Gnocchi with Sage and Lemon Sauce

Sage leaves have wonderful properties – as do all herbs – but they are particularly high in vitamin C when they are fresh. Sage has a very strong flavour so you don't need an abundance of it, otherwise you will overpower the dish. Dairy-free cheese is suitable for one-year-old toddlers and over but you may want to reduce the amount of herbs and lemon by half.

Makes 4–6 servings

GF WF DF N YF V OPTIONAL EF

Gnocchi

1kg/2lb 4oz floury organic potatoes, peeled and cubed
1 heaped teaspoon Orgran No Egg egg replacer and 2 tablespoons cold filtered water (or 1 organic free-range egg if not on an egg-free diet)
200g/1¾ cups potato flour
85g/3oz dairy-free margarine
15g/½oz finely chopped fresh sage leaves
Freshly ground black pepper
Extra potato flour for dusting
1 teaspoon fine salt (optional)

Sauce

3 heaped tablespoons dairy-free margarine
1 heaped teaspoon dried sage leaves
Finely grated rind of 1 unwaxed organic lemon

To serve – optional

15g/½oz shredded basil leaves
Grated dairy-free hard cheese or a yeast-free brand (see page 192 for brand and stockist) or finely grated pecorino cheese (sheep's cheese) if tolerated

Boil the potatoes until soft enough to mash, drain them and return them to the pan. Mash the potatoes and then mix in all the gnocchi ingredients and allow to cool. Dust your hands with the extra flour and shape the mixture into walnut-size pieces, working very lightly. When they are the correct size, press the back of a fork a little way into the gnocchi to decorate with the traditional ridges.

Bring a large pan of filtered water to the boil with a teaspoon of salt, if using, and drop the gnocchi into the boiling water in batches but make sure that you keep them apart. Cook them for about 1 minute or until they bob up to the top and float. Lift them out with a slotted spoon and place in a warmed bowl; keep them warm while cooking the rest of the mixture in batches in the same way.

Melt the margarine, with the sage leaves, in a small pan until bubbling then remove from the heat. Stir in the grated lemon and drizzle the sauce all over the gnocchi. Serve the gnocchi sprinkled with the shredded basil leaves and accompany the dish with a bowl of grated cheese.

 Vegetarian dishes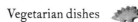

Tuscan Salad

This salad is rich in colour as well as texture, which is always a favourite with children. It is great for barbecues or al fresco lunches and you can easily double up on the ingredients if you have lots of hungry mouths to feed.

For the croûtons, make the bread recipe on page 186 or buy gluten-free white bread the day before you plan to make the recipe.

OPTIONAL

GF WF DF NF V   EF YF

Makes about 4 servings

1 red and 2 yellow organic sweet peppers, halved, stalk, pith and seeds removed

200ml/¾ cup cold pressed extra virgin olive oil, plus extra for brushing and drizzling

4 medium-sized ripe organic vine tomatoes

2 tablespoons cider vinegar (use lemon juice for yeast free)

1 organic garlic clove, crushed

Sea salt (optional) and freshly ground black pepper

4–6 very thick slices (depending on size) of day old gluten-free white bread or egg-free bread, crusts removed
  – check label for other allergens

100g/¾ cup pitted black olives* drained (in oil for yeast free)

A handful of fresh basil leaves

coeliacs please use gluten-free ingredients

Brush the peppers with a little oil and grill (broil) under the grill (broiler) or bake in a very hot oven until blistered with black spots and softened. Leave the peppers to cool and then scrape off the skins and discard. Keep one red pepper aside for the dressing and slice the remaining peppers into thick strips.

Score a large line across each tomato with a sharp knife, transfer to a bowl of boiling water and leave for 5 minutes or until the skins start to peel. Discard the water and carefully peel the skins off the tomatoes and discard. Slice the tomatoes in half, remove the core and seeds, which you can discard, and slice the tomatoes into thick strips.

In a food processor, blend the remaining pepper with the vinegar or lemon juice, garlic, salt, if using, pepper and oil until smooth.

Cut the slices of bread into bite-size cubes and shallow fry in a non-stick frying pan (skillet) over medium heat until they are golden on all sides. Drain the croûtons on absorbent kitchen paper.

To arrange the salad, divide the peppers, tomatoes, croûtons, olives and basil between the plates and drizzle with the dressing.

Chicken tikka wraps, p. 110

Fishcakes with polenta chips and tomato ketchup, pp. 104, 98

Halloween chicken in a pumpkin, p. 118

Easter chocolate nest, p. 176

Castle puddings, p. 148

Airy fairy cakes and cherry muffins , pp. 164, 169

Lemon and pine nut tarts and mini mince pies, pp. 162, 170

Animal cookies, p. 158

Baked Hedgehog Potatoes

It is always great fun for children to bake their own potatoes in a creative and inventive way. If it can be tolerated, you can substitute goat's or sheep's cheese for the dairy-free cheese.

Makes 4

4 × 255g/9oz organic baking potatoes, scrubbed clean
2 tablespoons cold pressed sunflower oil
1 organic garlic clove, peeled and crushed (size according to strength desired)
1 teaspoon chopped fresh rosemary or thyme leaves
Freshly ground black pepper
1–2 organic courgettes (zucchini), trimmed and cut into 12 thin slices
1–2 organic tomatoes (discard top and bottom), thinly cut into 12 slices
150g/5½oz packet dairy-free grated hard cheese or a yeast-free brand (see brand and stockist page 192)

Preheat the oven to 200°C/400°F/Gas mark 6.

Place the potatoes in the oven and cook for about 1 hour or until they are soft all the way through. Meanwhile, mix together the oil, garlic, rosemary and pepper.

Remove the potatoes from the oven and when they are cool enough, make 3 deep cuts widthways. Make sure you do not cut right through the potato or it will fall to pieces. Slot a slice of courgette (zucchini) and a slice of tomato into each of the 3 cuts in the potatoes.

Transfer the hot potatoes to a baking sheet. Press a good helping of grated cheese on top of each potato, drizzle with the oil mixture and bake for a further 20 minutes until the cheese is melted and bubbling and the vegetables are tinged with golden brown.

Macaroni Cheese

The type of flour that you use may change the amount of milk needed in this recipe because of the different absorbency levels. I use Wellfoods flour, which is very absorbent, so you may need to add a little more milk at a time until you have a smooth but runny sauce. If the sauce is thick the whole dish will be very gloopy and sticky!

Makes about 4 servings

GF WF DF EF NF V

255g/9oz packet gluten- and egg-free macaroni-style pasta
55g/2oz dairy-free margarine plus an extra 30g/1oz for the topping
55g/scant ½ cup gluten-free white flour mix
875ml/3½ cups organic unsweetened dairy-free milk (soya or rice)
1 teaspoon Dijon mustard*
2 teaspoons Worcestershire sauce*
150g/5½oz packet dairy-free Cheezly Cheddar-style grated cheese (see pages 192 for brands and stockists)
Sea salt (optional) and freshly ground black pepper
Freshly grated nutmeg
Optional – some teenagers may like a sprinkling of cayenne

* coeliacs please use gluten-free ingredients

Preheat the oven to 200°C/400°F/Gas mark 6.

Bring a pan of water to the boil and cook the macaroni according to the instructions on the packet. Drain, refresh briefly under cold running water and transfer to a suitable ovenproof baking dish. Keep covered with clingfilm (plastic wrap) while you make the sauce.

Melt the 55g/2oz of margarine in a pan over low heat, stir in the flour with a wooden spoon and let the mixture cook for about a minute. Increase the heat to medium and add the milk little by little, stirring constantly until you have incorporated all the milk and the sauce becomes smooth and thick. Now stir in the mustard, Worcestershire sauce and half the grated cheese and season to taste with salt, if using, pepper and nutmeg.

Pour the sauce over the macaroni, mix it all together and level off. Cover the surface with the remaining grated cheese and sprinkle with a little cayenne, if using, and then dot with little pieces of the extra margarine. Grill (broil) the macaroni for about 10 minutes or until golden and bubbling.

If you have made the macaroni a few hours in advance then bake in the oven for about 20 minutes until hot and bubbling.

Chickpea and Pasta Salad

Children love chickpeas (garbanzos), which seems very advanced to me as I did not like them until I was about 30! This is a tasty, filling and inexpensive salad that is great in the summer served with plenty of green and tomato salads – or even in winter served with baked potatoes and melted dairy-free cheese for hungry teenagers.

OPTIONAL

GF   WF   DF   NF   V   EF   YF

Makes about 4 servings

425g/15oz can organic chickpeas (garbanzos), without salt or sugar
250g/9oz packet gluten- and egg-free pasta shapes (not spaghetti or tagliatelle)
2 tablespoons cold pressed extra virgin olive oil
1 organic garlic clove, peeled and crushed
Sea salt (optional) and freshly ground black pepper
4–5 heaped tablespoons Granovita Mayola yeast- and egg-free mayonnaise or Tofutti Sour Supreme sour
    cream substitute (amount needed will vary according to pasta absorbency)
2 heaped tablespoons freshly chopped parsley, basil, coriander (cilantro) or mint leaves
1 large organic sweet red pepper, stalk, pith and seeds removed

Drain the chickpeas (garbanzos) and rinse under cold running water. Bring a pan of water to the boil and cook the pasta according to the instructions on the packet. Drain the pasta and briefly rinse under cold running water. Transfer the pasta to a warm serving bowl and add the chickpeas (garbanzos), oil and garlic. Season with a little salt, if using, and pepper and stir in the mayonnaise. Chop up the herbs and red pepper and mix them into the pasta salad.

You can chill the salad leftovers but serve it at room temperature.

Potato, Cheese and Parsley Pie

I make this at my parent's house in Norfolk, where they have a lovely kitchen garden and grow delicious parsley and potatoes. I could not resist putting them together in this cheap, cheerful and filling lunch dish. Serve it with plenty of green leafy vegetables, salads, or with a dish of roasted vegetables splashed with olive oil and fresh herbs.

Makes about 6 servings

GF   WF   DF   NF   V   OPTIONAL EF   YF

Pastry
255g/2 generous cups gluten-free flour mix, sifted
55g/2oz dairy-free margarine
55g/2oz vegetable shortening (Cookeen is good)
A little cold filtered water
Optional – 1 organic free-range egg if not on egg-free diet

Filling
About 1.2kg/2¾lb organic potatoes (you can judge how many you will need after you have peeled them – you may need more if they are old and have thick skins or less if the potatoes are new)
3 organic garlic cloves, peeled and crushed
4 tablespoons finely chopped fresh parsley
A pinch of freshly grated nutmeg
Optional – black pepper and sea salt
1 large or 2 medium organic onions, halved and finely sliced
250ml/1 cup soya cream
250ml/1 cup organic unsweetened soya milk
100g/3½oz dairy-free Cheddar-style grated Cheezly cheese (see stockists on page 192) – not for a yeast-free diet, instead use goat's or sheep's cheese if tolerated or omit altogether
About 55g/2oz dairy-free margarine

 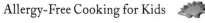

Preheat the oven to 200°C/400°F/Gas mark 6.

Make the pastry by mixing the flour, margarine and vegetable shortening together in a food processor, adding a little water at a time until the mixture resembles fine breadcrumbs. If using the egg, add it first and then as much water as you need to bind the dough into a ball. Wrap the pastry in clingfilm (plastic wrap) and chill for 30 minutes.

Slice the potatoes wafer thin, otherwise they will not cook through. I suggest using the slicing equipment in a food processor. Arrange a layer of potato slices over the base of a 33cm/12in gratin dish with some garlic, parsley, nutmeg and seasoning, if using, sprinkled all over. Cover with half of the onion slices and more of the potatoes and then a final layer of each. Each layer of potatoes should have a sprinkling of garlic, parsley, nutmeg and seasoning. Make sure that the potatoes don't hang over the edge of the dish or there will be nothing for the pastry to cling to. Arrange the potatoes lightly and in overlapping circles.

Pour over the cream and milk so that it is evenly distributed. Now sprinkle with all the cheese and dot with a few little bits of margarine.

Roll out the pastry on a floured surface into the shape and size needed to cover the dish, keeping the edges thick. Place it over the potatoes and crimp the edges with your fingertips. This way the pastry will not shrink.

Cut a small incision in the centre of the pie and transfer it to the centre of the oven. Bake the pie for about 55 minutes until the pastry is golden brown and the filling is soft and cooked right through the centre. The high temperature is needed at the start to ensure that the potatoes cook as well as the pastry but turn the temperature down to 190°C/375°F/Gas mark 5 after the first 30 minutes and cover the pastry very loosely with foil.

Remove the foil and let the pie cool down for about 5 minutes before serving.

Pile-High Pizza

Homemade pizza is not junk food when it is loaded with tomatoes and fresh vegetables, organic meats, chicken, herbs and garlic. A very good way to get your kids to eat lots of these goodies is to make the bases for them but to let them add the toppings. They will inevitably pile the pizza high with all the goodies and then feel that they have to eat it all as they chose it in the first place.

GF　WF　DF　EF　NF　V

Makes 4 pizzas

The pizza bases
400g/3½ cups gluten-free flour mix, plus extra for dusting and kneading
¼ teaspoon sea salt (optional)
1 teaspoon unrefined caster (superfine) sugar
15g/1 tablespoon gluten-free easy-bake-style yeast or fast-action dried yeast
300ml/1¼ cups tepid filtered water
A drizzle of cold pressed extra virgin olive oil

(alternatively, use 1 packet of Orgran Pizza mix and follow the instructions)

The sauce
1 tablespoon cold pressed extra virgin olive oil
425g/15oz can organic chopped tomatoes
2 tablespoons organic tomato purée (paste)
1 organic garlic clove, peeled and crushed
20g/¾ cup fresh basil leaves
Freshly ground black pepper

Topping suggestions
1 small bowl pitted black olives*, drained
1 small bowl (about 115g/4oz) dairy-free mozzarella-style slices or Cheddar-style grated cheese (see brands and stockists page 192) or use pecorino (sheep's cheese) or goat's cheese if not on a dairy-free diet
1 small bowl sliced organic sweet red peppers
1 small bowl sliced organic mushrooms (just wipe with a clean cloth)
1 small bowl sliced blanched organic courgettes (zucchini)
1 small bowl thinly sliced organic red onions
1 small bowl tiny blanched organic broccoli florets
1 small bowl halved organic baby vine tomatoes
1 small bowl organic frozen sweetcorn and peas

2 large non-stick baking sheets

* coeliacs please use gluten-free ingredients

Preheat the oven to 200°C/400°F/Gas mark 6.

Sift the flour into a big bowl and add the salt, if using. Stir in the sugar and yeast. Beat in the water using a wooden spoon and bring the dough together into a ball. You may need to add a little more warm water; different flours absorb varying amounts. Put the dough on a floured board and knead with floured hands for 6–10 minutes until it is smooth. Brush a large bowl with the oil, put the pizza dough into it and cover with a plate or another bowl. Leave the bowl in a warm, draught-free place until the dough has increased in size. This will take about an hour, depending on the temperature of your room. Alternatively, make up the pizza mix according to instructions.

Meanwhile, make the sauce. Warm the olive oil in a non-stick pan and tip the tomatoes into it. Stir in the tomato purée (paste), garlic and basil leaves. Season with pepper and increase the heat to medium. Cook the sauce for about 5 minutes until thickened and glossy.

Place the pizza dough on a floured board and flatten it with a rolling pin. Using a knife, divide it into four equal portions and roll out each portion on a floured board into a small circle. Place two pizza bases on each baking sheet. Press the pizza dough gently outwards with your fingers until it becomes a thin circle and neaten the edges. Brush all around the edges with a little more oil.

Arrange a line of little bowls filled with the olives, cheese and vegetables (or anything else that is healthy that your children will eat). Cover each pizza with the tomato sauce, going as near to the edges as you can and then place the trays in front of the bowls of goodies and let each child pile their pizza high. Bake the pizzas for about 15 minutes or until the crust is crisp and golden brown and the cheese (if used) is bubbling. Carefully slide the pizzas onto warm plates and serve them at a safe temperature.

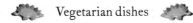 Vegetarian dishes

Polenta Chips with Tomato Ketchup

Fries in whatever form are always a hit with kids but these crunchy polenta chips are great if you have a child that cannot eat potatoes. They can soak up lots of healthy homemade ketchup and are great as a snack or can accompany grilled (broiled), baked or fried chicken, meat or vegetables. For a super-quick recipe that the kids can make themselves just buy an organic block of ready-made polenta*, cut it into chips and fry in the oil with the sage until crispy. Sprinkle lightly with the cheese when serving.

Makes about 4 servings

1 quantity Tomato Ketchup (see recipe page 102)

Chips

100g/3½oz instant 100% corn polenta

½ teaspoon finely chopped dried sage

30g/1oz very finely grated dairy-free Cheddar-style cheese or a yeast-free brand (see brands and stockists page 192) or goat's or sheep's cheese, if tolerated

15g/½oz dairy-free margarine

A pinch of salt and freshly ground black pepper (optional)

Cold pressed sunflower oil for shallow frying

* coeliacs please use gluten-free ingredients

Make the ketchup first.

Now prepare the polenta chips. Bring 250ml/1 cup of water to the boil in a medium-sized, non-stick saucepan. Remove the boiling water from the heat and quickly stir in the polenta and sage. Reduce the temperature to medium and return the pan to the heat for a couple of minutes, stirring constantly. Remove the polenta from the heat and stir in the cheese, margarine and the seasoning, if using.

Return the polenta to the pan and stir vigorously until it comes away from the sides of the pan and is smooth. While the polenta is still warm, spoon it onto a piece of non-stick baking parchment (wax paper) on a flat tray or board and shape it with your hands into a flattened ball. Spread it out evenly to make an oblong about 20.5 x 10 x 1cm/8 x 4 x ½in. If you make it larger, the chips may break up when you fry them. Cut the warm but solid polenta into 16 chunky chips. At this stage you can make them in advance and keep them in the refrigerator until needed.

Heat a little oil in a non-stick frying pan (skillet) and fry over high heat for about 2 minutes and then quickly turn them over and fry on the other side for another couple of minutes. As soon as they are golden and crispy, drain them on absorbent kitchen paper and serve immediately with a pool of tomato ketchup.

Cheesy Roulade

This roulade is a sort of flat cheese soufflé rolled around a mixture of fresh roasted vegetables. It can be served warm or you can make it a day in advance, chill it and serve with a jug of chilled tomato sauce.

OPTIONAL

Serves about 8

GF WF DF NF V YF

For the filling
400g/14oz thinly sliced organic courgettes (zucchini)

3 organic sweet red peppers, quartered, stalk, pith and seeds removed (or any other favourite vegetable combinations, sliced thinly)

A drizzle of cold pressed extra virgin olive oil

Fresh or dried thyme leaves

100g/3½oz soft Tofutti creamy cheese-style dip (see page 192 for stockist) or goat's/sheep's soft cheese if tolerated

A little extra dairy-free milk

Fine salt (optional) and freshly ground black pepper

2 tablespoons of either finely chopped fresh basil, coriander (cilantro) or parsley leaves

Roulade
30g/1oz dairy-free margarine, plus extra for greasing

2 tablespoons gluten-free flour mix

200ml/¾ cup organic unsweetened soya milk (or use rice, almond or oat milk depending on diet)

4 large organic free-range eggs, separated

2 heaped teaspoons Dijon mustard*

85g/3oz Cheddar-style dairy-free grated cheese, or a yeast-free brand (see brands and stockists on page 192), or hard goat's or sheep's cheese grated, if tolerated

1 teaspoon organic sesame seeds

500ml/2 cups of ready-made, allergy-free tomato sauce or make your favourite recipe

33 x 23cm/12 x 9in Swiss roll tin, greased and lined with non-stick baking parchment (wax paper)

1 extra sheet of baking parchment (wax paper)

*** coeliacs please use gluten-free ingredients**

Preheat the oven to 200°C/400°F/Gas mark 6.

Place the vegetables on a baking tray, drizzle with olive oil, sprinkle over the thyme and bake in the oven until browned at the edges, slightly blistered with black patches and soft all the way through.

Heat through your tomato sauce, transfer to a pouring jug and keep warm.

Using a wooden spoon, soften the creamy cheese in a small bowl with the extra milk, so that it becomes spreadable. Season with salt, if using, and pepper, mix in the chopped herbs and keep to one side.

Melt the margarine in a pan over low heat, add the flour and stir vigorously, cooking it for about a minute before gradually stirring in the milk. Increase the heat to medium and bring to the boil, stirring continuously. Cook for 1 minute. Remove the pan from the heat and season to taste with salt, if using, and pepper. Beat in the egg yolks, then the mustard and cheese.

Whisk the egg whites until stiff and fold into the cheese mixture. Pour into the prepared tin and quickly spread out evenly. Bake for about 10 minutes until well risen and firm to the touch.

If you haven't already taken the vegetables out of the oven it may be a good time to do so now, so that the peppers can cool down enough for you to peel off the blistered skins.

Lay a sheet of baking parchment (wax paper), the same size as the roulade, on a flat surface and sprinkle with the sesame seeds. Turn the roulade out, upside down, on to the paper and then peel off the paper from the roulade. Leave the roulade to cool for a couple of minutes then spread with the cream cheese mixture and cover evenly with the mixed vegetables.

Roll up the roulade, using the paper to help you – lift the far end and roll it quickly towards you. Slice off the ends and discard. Carefully transfer the roulade to a serving dish and serve it immediately with the warm tomato sauce.

Alternatively, you can let the roulade cool completely, spread with cheese and vegetables, roll and wrap the roulade tightly in the parchment (wax paper) and chill. Trim the ends off the roulade, cut into thick slices and serve with a chilled tomato sauce.

 Vegetarian dishes

Tomato Ketchup

This is such delicious ketchup – just like the real thing. You can wash and dry a ketchup bottle and refill it with this homemade version. Keep it sealed and chilled in the refrigerator for up to a week.

GF WF DF EF NF V

Makes about 4 servings

1 kg/2lb 4oz ripe organic vine tomatoes
3 teaspoons tarragon wine vinegar
3 tablespoons unrefined cane sugar
2 pinches each of cinnamon, freshly ground black pepper, sea salt, ground mace and allspice

Thickly slice the tomatoes, place in a pan with 2 tablespoons of water and cook for about 5 minutes, stirring frequently. Allow the tomatoes to cool and then liquidize them in a blender or food processor.

Sieve the sauce, return it to the pan and stir in the vinegar, sugar and spices. Bring the sauce to the boil and then reduce the heat and simmer until it has reduced to a thick sauce, the consistency of ready-made tomato ketchup. Allow the sauce to go cold. Pour the ketchup through a funnel into a sterilized bottle or spoon it into a jar, seal and store in the refrigerator.

Fish

Fishcakes and Fish Fingers

I have sneaked some iron-packed watercress into this recipe but you could use chopped fresh parsley leaves instead, which also contain iron as well as vitamin C. Choose which shape is suitable according to age – toddlers tend to prefer fingers as they can eat them with their hands, while teenagers and adults tend to like fishcakes.

For younger children use the egg-free version. For teenagers you can add a dash of cayenne pepper, salt and pepper to the flour mixture. Both the fishcakes and fish fingers freeze well.

OPTIONAL

GF	WF	DF	NF	EF	YF

Makes about 6 servings

About 30g/1oz dairy-free margarine and a little extra

455g/1lb fresh, skinned smoked haddock, cod or salmon fillet

Freshly ground black pepper and sea salt (optional)

565g/1¼lb organic potatoes, peeled, steamed and mashed, nothing added

2 heaped tablespoons chopped organic watercress leaves

Optional – 2 organic free-range eggs, lightly beaten

Gluten-free flour mix for dusting if using eggs, or rice flour for egg-free version

About ⅓ x 300g/10½oz packet Orgran all purpose gluten-, wheat- and yeast-free crumbs (excellent rice
   crumbs) or make you own white bread (see recipe page 186) or make an egg- and yeast-free bread such as
   Orgran and the following day make it into very fine breadcrumbs

Cold pressed extra virgin olive oil

Non-stick baking parchment (wax paper)

Preheat the oven to 180°C/350°F/Gas mark 4.

Grease a gratin dish with margarine and lay your fish fillets in it. Dot the fish with little pieces of the margarine, season with black pepper and cook in the oven for about 15 minutes. Leave the fish to cool, pile it on top of the mashed potato and mash together lightly. The fish must remain flaky and not be pulverized to a paste. Add the pepper, the salt, if using, and the watercress. Mash together lightly until well blended.

If you are not cooking the egg-free version, place four large plates in front of you and place the beaten eggs on the first, a heap of flour on the second and a pile of crumbs on the third – the last plate is for the finished product.

Flour your hands and pull off a fishcake- or fish finger-sized piece of the potato and fish mixture. Shape it, then dip it in the pile of flour. Shake off the excess, dip and roll the cake or finger in the beaten egg and then place on the plate of crumbs. Cover the fishcake or finger with lots of crumbs and pat gently. Place the finished article on the empty plate and repeat until all the mixture is used. For egg-free fishcakes or fingers, you only need two plates; one plate for a pile of rice flour, another for the prepared cakes or fingers. Simply dip and dust the fishcakes or fish fingers in a thick coating of rice flour.

At this point you can freeze the fishcakes or the fish fingers on a sheet of non-stick baking parchment (wax paper). When they are frozen, carefully wrap them up in clingfilm (plastic wrap) and return them to the deep freeze. Both the fishcakes and the fish fingers can be cooked from frozen.

Heat about 6 tablespoons of oil over medium heat in a non-stick frying pan (skillet) until hot. Cook the fishcakes or fish fingers until golden brown on both sides and serve with a big squirt of homemade tomato ketchup (see recipe on page 102).

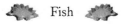 Fish

Fennel, Corn and Fish Pie

This is a popular fish pie with my teenage nephew and niece, William and Araminta, but for younger children you can omit the fennel and add cooked sweetcorn kernels and/or peas. As long as it is completely free of fish bones, then it is great mashed up and given to toddlers.

Makes about 6 servings

GF WF DF EF NF YF

Topping

1.1kg/2lb 8oz organic peeled potatoes, steamed and mashed by hand with dairy-free margarine and plenty of unsweetened organic soya milk or rice milk (it should be soft and spreadable but not sloppy)

A little extra dairy-free margarine

Pie mixture

740g/1lb 10oz boned, filleted cod or other white fish, cut into 2.5cm/1in-thick chunks

2 bulbs organic fennel, trimmed at base and top and of any tough layers

4 thin slices organic rindless smoked back bacon

3 heaped tablespoons frozen organic sweetcorn kernels, defrosted

Béchamel sauce

55g/2oz dairy-free margarine

55g/½ cup gluten-free flour mix

600ml/2½ cups organic unsweetened soya milk or rice milk

Sea salt (optional) and freshly ground black pepper

2 tablespoons finely chopped flat-leaf parsley

Preheat oven to 180°C/350°F/Gas mark 4.

Make the mashed potato topping as indicated in the ingredients list and keep it covered and warm until needed. Cut the cod into bite-sized chunks and put them in the bottom of a deep 33cm/12in ovenproof dish.

To make the béchamel sauce, melt the margarine in a saucepan, stir in the flour, heat gently for a minute and then gradually add the milk, stirring constantly until thickened. Add salt, if using, pepper and parsley and keep covered and warm until needed.

Cut the fennel into quarters vertically. Steam the quarters of fennel until just soft at their base, then lay them over the fish.

Snip the bacon into fine strips, fry until brown and crispy, drain the bits on absorbent kitchen paper and then sprinkle over the fennel and fish. Spoon the sweetcorn all over the fish and then pour over the béchamel sauce. It may not appear much, but cod exudes quite a lot of juice while cooking and you don't want it to be runny. Use a spatula to spread the fish with the mashed potato; furrow the surface of the potatoes with a fork and dot with a little extra margarine. Cook for 35–40 minutes until golden and bubbling.

Salmon Penne with Pine Nuts

If you have time, do try and find a bit of wild salmon for this recipe. It is so much tastier and of course it is not fed a diet that contains chemicals or preservatives. The texture is also much nicer as it is firmer than its farmed relative.

Makes about 4 servings

GF   WF   DF   EF   YF

255g/9oz gluten- and egg-free penne rigate (pasta quills)

250ml/1 cup soya cream

55g/2oz dairy-free margarine

1 small clove organic garlic, peeled and crushed

2 heaped teaspoons organic tomato purée (paste)

455g/1lb skinless, boneless salmon tail fillet

1 tablespoon cold pressed extra virgin olive oil

55g/2oz organic pine nuts

3 tablespoons ready-grated dairy-free Cheddar-style cheese, or a yeast-free brand (see brands and stockists page 192), or use goat's or sheep's cheese if it can be tolerated

Sea salt (optional) and freshly ground black pepper

Cook the pasta in a large pan of boiling water according to the instructions on the packet.

Meanwhile, pour the cream into a small pan and add the margarine and garlic. Stir in the tomato purée (paste) and heat gently.

Cut the salmon widthways into 1cm/½in-wide strips and fry the fish in the oil for a minute or two only until just cooked through. Do not turn the pieces over, as it will encourage them to break up. Transfer the fish to a large, warmed pasta bowl. In the same pan of oil, quickly fry the pine nuts until golden and then add to the salmon pieces.

Stir the cheese into the hot cream, add salt, if using, and pepper and remove from the heat. Drain the pasta and transfer to the pasta bowl. Pour the cream over, gently toss the pasta and serve immediately.

Poultry

Chicken Tikka Wraps

Super cool wraps – what every child wants in his or her lunchbox or on a picnic. Food wrapped in a parcel is always more scrummy. Wheat wraps are everywhere – supermarkets, snack bars, even the chiller cabinets in the pharmacy, but sadly there's not a gluten free one to be seen. You can freeze the tortillas, just reheat, cool and wrap.

Makes 6 tikka wraps and 6 extra tortillas for freezing

Tortillas

225g/2 cups gluten-free flour mix, plus extra for kneading and rolling dough

30g/2 tablespoons lard (hard white vegetable shortening)

A pinch of sea salt

185ml/¾ cup warm filtered water

Filling

(enough for 6 tortillas for 6 children – for 6 teenagers double this quantity of filling and fill all 12 tortillas)

3–4 medium-sized organic skinned chicken breasts, trimmed of fat

2 heaped teaspoons ground Tikka spice* (check label for allergens)

250ml/1 cup plain set organic soya yogurt (or goat's/sheep's yogurt if suitable)

Sea salt (optional) and freshly ground black pepper

1 teaspoon cold pressed sunflower oil

2 heaped tablespoons dairy-, nut-, yeast- and egg-free mayonnaise* (Granovita Mayola see page 195) or more if needed to make a binding sauce – alternatively use Tofutti Sour Supreme sour cream substitute, which is free of all the above

1 organic cos (Romaine) lettuce, finely shredded

Thin slices of peeled organic cucumber and tomatoes

1 heaped tablespoon chopped fresh parsley – alternatively use chopped fresh coriander (cilantro) leaves for older kids

* coeliacs please use gluten-free ingredients

Allergy-Free Cooking for Kids

Make the tortillas about 2 hours before you plan to serve the finished dish. Sift the flour into a medium bowl and rub in the lard (shortening) with your fingertips until it resembles fine breadcrumbs. Make a well in the centre of the mixture. Dissolve the salt in the warm water and then pour it into the well. Mix with your hands, gradually incorporating the surrounding flour mixture to make a soft dough. Turn this out onto a floured board and knead for 2–3 minutes, then place in a floured bowl, cover with clingfilm (plastic wrap) and leave to rest for 1 hour.

Meanwhile, chop the chicken into bite-size diagonal pieces and toss in a bowl with the spice, yogurt and oil and sprinkle with a little pepper. Cover and marinate in the refrigerator for at least 30 minutes. Spread the chicken out over a non-stick baking tray and grill (broil) until cooked through and slightly browned in patches on both sides. Leave the chicken to get cold on the tray.

Turn the dough out onto a floured surface, knead for 1 minute and then divide into 12 small balls. Keep these covered under clingfilm (plastic wrap) while you make each tortilla in turn. Flour the surface again and roll out one of the balls to an 18cm/7in paper-thin round, giving the dough a quarter turn each time you roll it. Repeat with the remaining dough balls, covering each finished tortilla with clingfilm (plastic wrap) so that it does not dry out.

Heat a 20.5cm/8in non-stick frying pan (skillet) over medium-high heat. Add a tortilla and cook for 30–40 seconds until bubbles appear on the surface and the underside is speckled with brown. Do not overcook or the tortilla will be too dry to roll. Slide the tortilla onto a plate and cover with a piece of baking parchment. Cook the remaining tortillas in the same way, stacking them on the plate with a piece of parchment between each. Set them aside while you prepare the filling.

When the chicken is cold, toss it in a bowl with the mayonnaise – if you are catering for hungry teenagers, you may need a little extra yogurt as well. It should make a firm filling which won't drip and ooze but won't be dry and solid either. You can make much more sauce if the tortillas are being eaten at home on a plate than if the tortillas are being taken in a lunchbox or on a picnic.

Spoon the chicken filling onto one side of the centre of the tortilla, sprinkle with the chopped lettuce, slices of cucumber and tomato and the herbs and wrap the unfilled half around the filling. If you are packing the tikka wraps in a lunchbox or taking them on a picnic, wrap them in non-stick baking parchment (wax paper).

Corn and Watercress Fritters with Sticky Drumsticks

This combination is great because younger children can eat both the corn fritters and the chicken drumsticks with their fingers. For older children, it is a popular and easy meal when their friends come round. Marinate the chicken for as long as possible but keep it covered and chilled.

Makes 4–8 servings

The marinade and drumsticks

80ml/⅓ cup organic Tamari soy sauce or another gluten-free sauce

2 tablespoons sesame oil

5cm/2in piece organic root ginger, peeled and grated

4 organic garlic cloves, peeled and crushed

Juice of 1 unwaxed organic orange

2 teaspoons organic blackstrap molasses

8 organic chicken drumsticks with their skins on

8 fritters

170g/6oz drained weight of canned organic sweetcorn kernels or use 1 cup of cooked and drained frozen or fresh kernels

4 heavily trimmed and finely chopped organic spring onions (salad onions)

4 tablespoons freshly chopped watercress leaves and finest part of the stalks

3 tablespoons gluten-free flour mix

½ teaspoon gluten-free baking powder

A good pinch of unrefined cane sugar

1 organic free-range egg, separated

60ml/¼ cup soya cream

A little freshly ground black pepper and a tiny bit of sea salt (optional)

Extra virgin olive oil for shallow frying

  Allergy-Free Cooking for Kids

Preheat the oven to 180°C/350°F/Gas mark 4.

Simply mix the marinade ingredients in the dish you are going to cook the chicken in and lay the drumsticks in it. Cover the dish and leave in the fridge. Turn the drumsticks once or twice to marinate evenly. Bring the drumsticks back to room temperature before cooking but keep them away from any source of heat, so as to avoid any risk of food poisoning.

Place the dish of drumsticks in the oven and cook for about 30–40 minutes, basting occasionally. Insert a skewer to see if they are cooked through. No blood should run from them. Remove the drumsticks from the oven and leave them to cool while you make the fritters.

In a bowl, mix the prepared corn, spring onions (salad onions) and the chopped watercress. Stir in the flour, baking powder and sugar and then mix in the egg yolk, cream and seasoning, if using.

Beat the egg white until it forms firm peaks, then fold into the prepared mixture. Heat 3–4 tablespoons of olive oil in a large non-stick frying pan (skillet) over a medium heat. Drop tablespoonfuls of the batter into the oil, squashing them flat, and fry for 2–3 minutes each side until puffed and golden. Drain on kitchen paper. Serve immediately with the chicken drumsticks and a big bowl of mixed salad or freshly cooked green vegetables.

Chicken and Pesto Pasta Shapes

This recipe for pesto is easy and can be used for any style of pasta. Another good idea for using pesto is to mix it into the scooped out mashed potato of a baked potato, place the mixture back in the skin and then grill (broil) it until golden – quick, easy and delicious.

Serves 4–6

4 organic skinless and trimmed chicken breasts (or for speed buy the ready-cooked breasts)

A little cold pressed extra virgin olive oil

Sea salt (optional) and freshly ground black pepper

255g/9oz packet gluten- and egg-free pasta shapes (spirals or bows are good)

Optional – a little crushed organic garlic

Pesto

35g/1¾oz fresh basil leaves

8 tablespoons cold pressed extra virgin olive oil

2 heaped tablespoons organic pine nuts

100g/3½oz Cheddar-style grated dairy-free cheese or a yeast-free brand (see page 192 for brand & stockists)

Preheat the oven to 200°C/400°F/Gas mark 6.

Put the chicken breasts in an ovenproof dish, brush with a little oil and dust with salt, if using, and pepper. Add 250ml/1 cup of cold filtered water to the dish, cover it with foil and bake in the oven for about 25 minutes or until the chicken is cooked all the way through.

Meanwhile, bring a pan of water to the boil and cook the pasta according to the instructions on the packet. When the chicken is cooked, remove from the oven and lift off the foil so that the chicken cools slightly.

Put all the pesto ingredients in the food processor and whiz until it becomes a fine glossy sauce. Chop up the chicken into bite-size pieces and cover briefly with the foil while you drain the pasta. Toss the pasta in a warm serving bowl with the pesto and a little garlic, if using. Fold in the chopped chicken, season with a little freshly ground black pepper and serve immediately.

Bashed-Up Chicken

This treatment of chicken breasts is a marvellous way of getting all the pent up energy or aggression out of a teenager! Let them bash away but not so much they make holes in the flesh – keep it even and intact.

Serves 4

4 large boneless, skinless organic chicken breasts
8 thin slices prosciutto
8 fresh sage leaves
2 tablespoons gluten-free flour mix
Sea salt (optional) and freshly ground black pepper
3 tablespoons cold pressed extra virgin olive oil
30g/1oz dairy-free margarine
250ml/1 cup clear apple juice (or sweet cider for grown-ups)
Finely grated rind of ½ an unwaxed organic lemon
1 tablespoon finely chopped fresh flat-leaf parsley

4 wooden skewers

On a clean chopping board, cut down the length of each chicken breast along one side and open it out flat. Place each breast between 2 sheets of clingfilm (plastic wrap) and flatten by bashing with a rolling pin. Remove the clingfilm (plastic wrap).

Place a slice of proscuitto and a sage leaf on each piece of chicken and fold the chicken back over into its original shape. Secure each breast down the middle with a wooden skewer.

Season the flour with salt, if using, and freshly ground black pepper, then press each breast into the mixture to coat evenly.

Heat the oil in a large, deep frying pan (skillet) and cook the chicken over high heat for about 3 minutes on each side, until golden brown. The chicken should be slightly undercooked; transfer it to a plate and add the margarine to the pan (skillet). When it is frothy, add the apple juice or cider and lemon rind and bring to the boil. Allow to bubble for 1 minute, then return the chicken to the pan, spooning over the juices, and cook for 5 minutes on each side.

Place each chicken breast on a plate, spoon the juices over the top, sprinkle with the parsley and serve immediately.

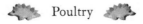

Chicken in Organic Crisps

Lucy James and I used this recipe in Merribel when we were chalet girls over 20 years ago and we still make it, as it is reliably popular with children and teenagers alike. The only concession to modernity that this recipe has undergone is the use of reduced-salt, organic crisps with their skins on.

Makes 6 servings

140–150g/5–6oz packet allergy-free organic reduced-salt potato crisps (chips), preferably the type with the skins on
3 tablespoons chopped fresh parsley
2 organic garlic cloves, peeled and crushed
3 tablespoons softened dairy-free margarine
Freshly ground black pepper
6 organic chicken breasts, trimmed and skins removed

Preheat the oven to 190°C/375°F/Gas mark 5.

Crush the crisps in a bowl. In another bowl, mix the parsley, garlic, margarine and pepper together until blended and soft and then gently fold in the crisps. Lay the chicken breasts on a non-stick baking tray and pat the mixture all over the chicken breasts. Cook them for about 50 minutes, depending on the size.

As soon as the chicken is cooked through, remove from the oven and serve with plenty of vegetables or salads.

Chicken Nuggets with Tomato Ketchup

The tomato ketchup makes up in vitamins for the fried breadcrumb coating and, if you use organic chicken, it is nutritious enough not to be classed as junk food. For convenience, you can freeze the nuggets ready to thaw and bake when you need them. The ketchup can be stored in a sealed jar for a week in the refrigerator.

Makes about 4 servings

1 quantity Tomato Ketchup (see recipe page 102)

Nuggets

85g/1½ cups homemade fine allergy-free white breadcrumbs or Orgran All Purpose crumbs, which are made from rice and are absolutely brilliant

Sea salt (optional) and freshly ground black pepper

2 organic free-range eggs (if not on an egg-free diet), lightly beaten or ⅓ x 300g/10½oz jar Granovita Mayola or use another egg-free mayonnaise but check that it is yeast free

4 skinned and trimmed organic chicken breasts

Extra virgin olive oil for shallow frying

Make the ketchup recipe and store until needed.

Put the crumbs in a shallow bowl and season with salt, if using, and pepper. Beat the eggs in another shallow bowl. Flatten the chicken with your hands and cut into bite-size chunks. Dip the chicken pieces in the egg and then coat them in the crumbs. If you cannot use eggs, simply coat the chicken pieces in a thin layer of egg-free mayonnaise, then dip the nuggets in the crumbs.

Heat the oil in a pan and fry the nuggets over high heat until they are brown on both sides and completely cooked through. Drain on absorbent kitchen paper and serve immediately, accompanied by plenty of green vegetables or salad and the ketchup.

Halloween Chicken in a Pumpkin

It is hard work carving out a pumpkin, which is why I always pass this task on to young volunteers. The end result is really fun for Halloween or just as a party piece in the autumn (fall).

Makes about 8 servings

3.8kg/8lb –9lb whole pumpkin, top sliced off and reserved

2 whole, cooked, medium-sized (about 1kg/2lb 2oz each) chickens* from the deli (or cook your own)

55g/2oz dairy-free margarine

4 heaped tablespoons gluten-free flour mix

600ml/2½ cups organic soya milk or rice milk (you can use almond milk if not on a nut-free diet)

2 teaspoons allergy-free vegetable bouillon/stock powder

250ml/1 cup soya cream

Sea salt (optional) and freshly ground black pepper

A little freshly grated nutmeg

2 heaped tablespoons of finely chopped fresh parsley leaves

* coeliacs please use gluten-free ingredients
(check chicken has not been basted in a gluten or wheat product)

Preheat the oven to 200°C/400°F/Gas mark 6.

Discard the pith and pips in the pumpkin. Carefully scrape out the inside of the pumpkin, discarding the flesh. Work your way round the inside until you have a rim of pumpkin flesh all the way round of about 2.5cm/1in – this is so that you don't chip or break the skin. This will also help support the filling and ensure that the whole thing doesn't collapse. Use the flesh for soup or a mash. Place the pumpkin on a large ovenproof serving dish.

Remove the skin from the cooked chickens and discard. Carve the chickens on a clean board, cut all the meat into bite-size pieces and set aside.

In a large non-stick pan, melt the margarine over low heat. Increase the heat to medium, stir in the flour and gradually stir in the milk. Beat the sauce until smooth and add the bouillon/stock powder, cream, pepper and nutmeg and bring to the boil. Remove from the heat, stir in the chicken pieces and parsley and adjust the seasoning if necessary with salt, if using, and pepper.

Fill the pumpkin with the chicken mixture and cover tightly with the pumpkin lid. Bake in the oven, in the ovenproof dish, for about 2 hours until the pumpkin is softened and the chicken is bubbling. You will not be eating the pumpkin, just the filling. Lift off the pumpkin lid and give the filling a good mix with a fork so that any juices that have seeped out of the pumpkin are thoroughly combined with the white sauce. If the sauce is too thick, add a little extra milk, stir and return to the oven for 10 minutes. Serve the pumpkin from the dish with either baked potatoes or rice.

Roast Turkey with Rocket and Potato Stuffing

This stuffing is great for the Christmas or Easter turkey and makes a nice change from the inevitable bread and sausage meat stuffing you usually get on these occasions. In this recipe, the stuffing is placed under the skin rather than inside the bird.

Serves 6–8

Stuffing

4 tablespoons cold pressed extra virgin olive oil

1 large organic onion, finely chopped

900g/2lb organic potatoes, peeled and cut into small cubes

4 large organic garlic cloves, crushed

1 tablespoon Herbes de Provence or mixed dried herbs

24 pitted black olives, in oil not vinegar, drained

2 large handfuls/2 cups gluten- and yeast-free breadcrumbs

20g/¾oz organic rocket (arugula) leaves

Finely grated rind of 1 unwaxed organic lemon

Sea salt (optional) and freshly ground black pepper

4.6kg/10lb 14oz prepared organic free-range turkey or an extra large family organic free-range chicken

Optional

• Plenty of rindless organic streaky smoked bacon rashers

• Herbes de Provence or mixed dried herbs

• Water, a little apple juice and allergy-free bouillon/stock powder

• A couple of bay leaves, some sliced onion and carrot

• Some pure cornflour (cornstarch) dissolved in cold water

Follow the temperature guides in your favourite recipe book for cooking your size turkey or a family-size chicken. This size of turkey took me 2¾ hours to cook in a hot oven.

To make the stuffing: Heat half the oil in a frying pan (skillet), add the chopped onion, finely diced potato and garlic and sauté until softened and translucent. Add the herbs and olives and stir to coat. Now add the remaining oil and the breadcrumbs and continue cooking until the crumbs are golden. Test the potatoes with a skewer – they should remain cubed and be almost cooked through. Remove from the heat, stir in the rocket (arugula) and the lemon rind, season and leave to cool.

In order to stuff the turkey, carefully ease the skin away from the breast, using a sharp knife to start with. Be careful not to cut the skin or it will split during cooking. Using a clean hand, wriggle under the skin and up to the top of the bird, easing the skin away from the flesh. Make enough room down the sides of the turkey as well. Pack all the stuffing in – if you are using a smaller bird you can stuff the remainder inside.

Place the stuffed turkey in a large roasting tin and roast in your favourite way until cooked through. I wrap lots of bacon round the turkey, sprinkle it with Herbes de Provence and freshly ground black pepper and loosely wrap with kitchen foil. I then add some bay leaves, onion, carrot and bouillon/stock powder to the pan and enough water or apple juice to come one-third of the way up the pan – this makes a delicious gravy and keeps the bird moist. I remove the foil for the last half hour of roasting time so that the bacon and skin is crispy and golden.

Let the turkey cool for 5 minutes before lifting it out of the pan and onto a carving board. Allow it to cool for another 5 minutes. Use the pan juices in the normal way to make your favourite gravy. You can thicken it with dissolved cornflour (cornstarch). Serve with plenty of traditional vegetables. It is also delicious with mashed sweet potato.

Meat

Toad in the Hole

My favourite story is The Wind and the Willows – its enduring charm still calms and restores me when I'm frazzled. It's not surprising then that I can't see the word toad without immediately thinking of him and his adventures. Anyway, back to the recipe! Do swap the sausages for roasted root vegetables sometimes, as it is much more nutritious. For a baby or toddler who can chew, use very small pieces of chopped up roasted root vegetables but no sausage, and moisten with a little water.

Makes 8–10

Batter

115g/1 cup gluten-free flour mix, sieved

A pinch of sea salt (optional)

2 heaped teaspoons Orgran No Egg egg replacer and 4 tablespoons water or as instructed on your packet (or 2 organic free-range eggs if not on a dairy-free diet)

300ml/1¼ cups organic unsweetened soya milk or rice milk

8–10 gluten-free organic sausages, check label for other allergens (see brands and stockists page 192) – use thin sausages for young kids, thicker sausages for older kids **OR**

500g/1lb 2oz organic root vegetables such as swede, parsnip, carrot or beetroot, washed, trimmed, peeled and cut into batons for older kids, or tiny dice for babies and toddlers

12-bun muffin tray, greased with a little oil

Preheat the oven to 200°C/400°F/Gas mark 6.

First make the batter. Mix the flour with the salt, if using, and make a well in the centre. Mix the egg replacer and water into the flour and gradually incorporate about half the milk. Now whisk in the remaining milk until there are bubbles on top. If using eggs, pour these into the well, incorporate into the flour and then only add as much milk as is necessary to obtain a smooth batter. Leave the batter to stand for 20 minutes.

Meanwhile, lightly bake the sausages in the preheated oven until just cooked through but pale in colour. Cool and cut each thin one in half but leave the thick ones whole.

Brush a little oil all over each bun mould and arrange 2 halves or 1 thick sausage jauntily in each one. Put the tin into the oven and heat for about 3 minutes. Transfer the batter into a jug for easy pouring.

Take the tin out of the oven and very quickly pour batter into each bun mould to about half way. Return the tray, equally quickly, to the oven and for about 25 minutes or until well risen and crisp (the batter does soften by the time the Toad in the Hole is served and ready to eat).

For the vegetarian version, lightly steam the vegetables then arrange the batons at a jaunty angle in each bun mould and follow the remainder of the recipe. For babies and toddlers just spoon in the chopped vegetables and continue with the recipe.

Spaghetti Carbonara Style

Some kids just cannot eat mushrooms and I have some sympathy with them, as I can't eat them either. In this recipe, the mushrooms are replaced with spring onions (salad onions) and mangetout (snow peas), or petits pois and sweetcorn. Older kids will probably prefer the first combination, while younger kids, who seem to prefer sweeter vegetables, will enjoy the peas and corn.

Makes 4–6 servings

250ml/1 cup soya cream

½ organic garlic clove, peeled and cut in half

Sea salt (optional)

20 trimmed organic mangetout (snow peas), sliced in half vertically and 4 washed organic spring onions (salad onions), heavily trimmed and finely sliced or 125g/1 cup cooked organic frozen petits pois and 125g/1 cup cooked organic frozen sweetcorn kernels

8 rashers rindless organic back or streaky bacon (or bacon bits* if in a hurry)

A little cold pressed extra virgin olive oil

255g/9oz gluten- and egg-free spaghetti

1 large organic free-range egg yolk (omit the egg for an egg-free diet)

55g/2oz dairy-free grated Cheddar-style cheese or a yeast-free brand (see page 192 for brand and stockists) or a goat's/sheep's cheese if not on a dairy-free diet

Freshly ground black pepper

30g/1oz dairy-free margarine

1–2 heaped tablespoons chopped fresh parsley (according to age group)

* coeliacs don't use ready cooked bacon bits unless gluten-free

In a small pan, heat the cream with the garlic over low heat, so that it has time to infuse.

Cook the pasta in boiling water until just al dente (only adding salt for older children). Meanwhile, blanch the mangetout (snow peas) in a small pan of boiling water, drain and keep to one side. Fry the bacon until crispy in a non-stick frying pan (skillet) for a few minutes and once some of the liquid has evaporated from the bacon, add the oil and cook until crispy.

Let the bacon rashers cool on some absorbent kitchen paper. Briefly fry the spring onions (salad onions) in the bacon oil and then transfer to a large warm serving bowl. Cut the bacon into tiny pieces and add to the onions in the bowl. (Alternatively, if you are using the bacon bits, fry them with a little olive oil and once golden, add the onions and cook until the bacon is crispy).

Drain the pasta in a colander and return to the pan. Pour in a little olive oil, stirring and tossing. Return to a very low heat on the hob, add the mangetout (snow peas) and toss together.

Remove the garlic pieces from the warm cream and discard them. In a small bowl beat the egg, if using, with the cream, grated cheese and some pepper and then pour the mixture into the pasta, toss again with the margarine and heat through for about a minute.

Combine the pasta mixture with the bacon and onions and serve immediately, sprinkled with a little chopped parsley. If you are using petits pois and sweetcorn just cook them until tender, as you normally would, drain them, add to the pasta and follow the remainder of the recipe.

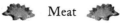

Yeast-Free Pizza

This recipe is basically soda bread with a delicious topping but it is a useful recipe if you don't want to use fresh or dried yeast. Choose your mixture of toppings according to taste and food sensitivities – you can also use the Pile-High Pizza ideas on page 96.

OPTIONAL

GF   WF   EF   NF   YF   V

Makes six 15cm/6in pizzas

Pizza base

450g/4 generous cups gluten-free white flour mix

1 teaspoon unrefined caster (superfine) sugar

1 heaped teaspoon gluten-free bicarbonate of soda (baking soda)

1 teaspoon sea salt

About 500ml/2 cups buttermilk (variable due to flour absorbency)

Topping

6 Toulouse gluten-free sausages (available at Sainsbury's) or other allergy-free organic sausages – vegetarians choose suitable vegetarian alternatives

425g/15oz can organic chopped tomatoes

2 heaped tablespoons organic tomato purée (paste)

1 teaspoon mixed dried herbs

Freshly ground black pepper

100g/3½oz pack grated buffalo mozzarella, Parmesan or pecorino shavings or dairy-free Tofutti mozzarella-style cheese slices or Florentino Parmazano (stockists see page 192) if preferred

A drizzle of cold pressed extra virgin olive oil

2 large non-stick baking trays

Preheat the oven to 190°C/375°F/Gas mark 5.

First cook the sausages until well browned on all sides and cooked through. You can either grill (broil) them or fry them in a very little oil in a frying pan (skillet).

Meanwhile, make the base. Sift the dry ingredients into a bowl, make a well and pour in the buttermilk, bit by bit, mixing until you get a soft but not wet or sticky dough (you may not need to use all the buttermilk). Turn the dough out onto a floured board, knead briefly for a few seconds to tidy it up, then roll out into six 15cm/6in rounds. Place three on each baking tray and neaten the edges.

In a bowl, mix the canned tomatoes with the tomato purée (paste), herbs and pepper and spread the mixture evenly over each pizza. Slice up the sausages and arrange them over the top of the tomato mixture and sprinkle each pizza with the cheese. Drizzle with a little oil and bake for about 15 minutes until the pizzas are golden and bubbling.

Lamb Moussaka

A girlfriend of mine, who has four stepchildren to cook for, produced this delicious moussaka for us all one night, and having remembered that I am allergic to aubergines (eggplant) cleverly used courgettes (zucchini) instead. I was so impressed that I have taken the idea and made it dairy free as well.

OPTIONAL

Makes 4–6 servings

GF   WF   DF   NF   YF

Mince

2 medium organic onions, finely chopped

500g/1lb 2oz lean minced (ground) organic lamb

1 tablespoon cold pressed extra virgin olive oil

Sea salt (optional) and freshly grated black pepper

1 organic garlic clove, peeled and crushed

1 heaped teaspoon Herbes de Provence or mixed herbs

2 tablespoons pure cornflour (cornstarch) dissolved in a little water

250ml/1 cup carrot juice

400g/14oz can organic chopped tomatoes

Filling and topping

900g/2lbs organic courgettes (zucchini), trimmed and thinly sliced

Cold pressed extra virgin olive oil

250ml/1 cup soya cream

2 large organic free-range eggs, beaten

115g/4oz dairy-free Cheddar-style grated cheese or a yeast-free brand (see brand and stockists page 192)

Freshly grated nutmeg

Preheat the oven to 180°C/350°F/Gas mark 4.

Heat the oil in a pan, add the onions and lamb and cook over a medium until the meat has browned all over. Season the mince with salt and pepper, add the garlic and herbs and simmer for a few minutes. Stir in the dissolved cornflour (cornstarch), mix in the carrot juice and simmer for a few minutes before adding the tomatoes. Simmer at bubbling point for about 20 minutes.

Meanwhile, make the topping. Fry the courgettes (zucchini) in a deep frying pan (skillet) with plenty of oil. When they are golden on both sides and cooked through, drain them on absorbent kitchen paper and set aside until needed. In a small bowl, mix the cream with the eggs and cheese and season with pepper and grated nutmeg.

Lay one-third of the cooked courgettes (zucchini) over the bottom of a deep ovenproof dish and cover them with half the mince. Spread another layer of courgettes (zucchini) over the mince and cover with the remaining mince. Finally, arrange the last of the courgettes (zucchini) in another layer and top with the cream sauce. Bake in the oven for about 35 minutes until golden and bubbling.

Cold desserts

Raspberry Ripple Ice Cream

Get the children to pick the raspberries and then whip up this sumptuous ice cream for them as a reward for their good deed. I normally make double rations so that it fills a 3 litre (3 quart) plastic container. You can make it a couple of weeks in advance for a party and then serve it accompanied by loads more fresh raspberries.

Makes 4–6 servings

Ice cream

600ml/scant 2½ cups organic unsweetened soya milk

1 vanilla pod, split lengthways or use pure vanilla extract to taste when the custard is cooling

250g/1⅓ cups unrefined caster (superfine) sugar

7 organic free-range egg yolks

2 heaped teaspoons pure cornflour (cornstarch)

500ml/2 cups soya cream

Ripple

220g/2 cups organic raspberries, plus extra to serve

55g/⅓ cup unrefined caster (superfine) sugar

1 tablespoon lemon juice

Put the milk and vanilla pod into a saucepan and bring to the boil. Remove the pan from the heat, let the milk cool for 30 minutes and then discard the vanilla pod.

Beat the sugar, egg yolks and cornflour (cornstarch) in a bowl with a wooden spoon until smooth and then pour in the vanilla milk. Transfer to a saucepan and heat gently, stirring continuously until you have a thin custard (too much heat and the custard will separate). Liquidize, transfer to a bowl, cool and then chill for an hour.

Meanwhile, make the ripple mixture. Put the raspberries, sugar, lemon juice and 1 tablespoon of cold filtered water into a saucepan. Bring to the boil, reduce the heat and simmer until soft. Push the mixture through a non-metal sieve into a bowl, discard the pips and chill the purée.

Stir the cream into the cold custard and pour into your ice cream maker. Churn and freeze according to the instructions. You may need to do this in two batches – if so, then store the first batch in the deep freeze until needed.

Remove the ice cream from the ice cream maker and spread one-third of the mixture into a shallow square or rectangular container. Mark parallel, deep, uneven furrows in the ice cream with a blunt knife, then pipe the raspberry purée into the furrows. Gently spread over another layer of ice cream until all the ice cream and raspberry mixture has been used. The final stripes of ripple can be as wittily wobbly as your children care to make them! Freeze the ice cream until it is set firm and then seal, label it and return to the freezer until needed.

To serve the ice cream, leave it to soften at room temperature and then scoop it out of the container. Alternatively, you can line the container with clingfilm (plastic wrap) so that you can turn it out onto a serving dish, surround with raspberries and serve it in slices.

Chunky Monkey Chocolate Ice Cream

I keep a double ration of this ice cream in the deep freeze so that it is always at hand for impromptu lunches or teas. I tend to keep it for special treats and opt for fruit-laden ice creams on a more regular basis.

Makes about 4 servings

4 large organic free-range egg yolks
1 heaped teaspoon pure cornflour (cornstarch)
4 heaped tablespoons unrefined cane sugar
300ml/1¼ cups organic unsweetened soya milk
3 tablespoons organic dairy-free cocoa powder*, sieved
250ml/1 cup soya cream
55g/2oz dairy- and nut-free dark chocolate chips* or chopped pieces of dairy- and nut-free dark chocolate*

* coeliacs please use gluten-free ingredients

Mix the egg yolks, cornflour (cornstarch) and sugar together in a bowl. Gradually add the milk. Transfer the mixture to a non-stick saucepan and cook over a low heat, stirring most of the time until thick – but do not boil. Remove the pan from the heat and stir in the cocoa powder and cream. Sieve the custard into a bowl and leave to cool.

When the mixture is cold and the ice cream maker is ready, mix in the chocolate chips or pieces and churn in the machine until frozen but still soft enough to scrape out of the mixer. Place in a container, seal and freeze until needed. Alternatively, serve immediately with suitable allergy-free cookies.

Super Cheat's Berry Ice Cream

This recipe uses dairy-free yogurt to make an instant ice cream for families with an ice cream maker. It takes just 30 minutes from start to finish.

Makes about 4 servings

GF   WF   DF   EF   NF   YF   V

500g/2 cups dairy-free berry-flavoured yogurt (Provamel organic soya Yofu summer fruits is good)
130g/4½oz fresh organic blueberries

Prepare and chill the ice cream maker for 5 minutes or as instructed. Mix and stir the Yofu and berries together in a bowl and scrape into the chilled ice cream bowl.

Churn until soft frozen and serve immediately.

DO NOT FREEZE AND DO NOT TRY AND MAKE HALF THE QUANTITY. You can make double the quantity. Serve in fun glasses with suitable cookies or more berries.

 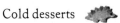

Chilled Vanilla Cheesecake

I had despaired of ever eating a cheesecake again until I came across the Tofutti range of cream cheeses. I can now make successful cheesecakes and various delicious cheese dips.

You can make this cheesecake decorated with bananas and served with the chocolate fudge sauce. Alternatively, decorate the cheesecake with any of the following: sliced strawberries, whole raspberries or blackberries, peeled and sliced peaches or nectarines, and serve with a coordinating fruit purée.

Makes one 23cm/9in cheesecake

GF WF DF V   OPTIONAL NF YF

Crust
150g/5½oz gluten-, yeast-, nut- and dairy-free digestive biscuits
150g/5½oz flavoured gluten-, dairy-, yeast- and nut-free biscuits (such as ginger, lemon, chocolate or coconut if not on a nut-free diet)
85g/3oz dairy-free margarine, melted
85g/3oz unrefined demerara sugar
Optional – ½ teaspoon ground cinnamon for chocolate- or plain-flavoured crumbs

Cheesecake
2 x 225g/8oz tubs gluten- and dairy-free Original Tofutti Creamy Smooth cream-style cheese
2 teaspoons pure vanilla extract
3 tablespoons soya cream
3 tablespoons unrefined caster (superfine) sugar
11.7g sachet/1 tablespoon gelatine powder dissolved in 150ml/½ cup plus 1 tablespoon of boiling water, or the vegetarian equivalent
2 organic free-range egg whites, stiffly beaten

To serve
Chocolate or Carob Fudge Sauce (see recipe on page 141) and 2 bananas, thinly sliced and tossed in a little lemon juice **OR**
Fruit sauce and glaze – mixed berries (fresh or frozen raspberries, strawberries or blackberries), a dash of rosewater, 3–4 tablespoons of suitable pipless jam (jelly)

23cm/9in spring-form, non-stick cake tin lined with non-stick baking parchment (wax paper) if you want to turn the cheesecake out onto a plate

Preheat oven to 180°C/350°F/Gas mark 4.

Make the crust first. Break up the biscuits and process them in a food processor until they resemble coarse breadcrumbs. In a small pan, heat the margarine, sugar and cinnamon, if using, until melted and then pour in the biscuit crumbs and mix thoroughly. Press the crumb mixture into the lined tin and press down until it is flat and even. Bake in the oven for about 20 minutes; remove from the oven and leave to cool.

When the base is cold make the filling. Place the first four ingredients for the cheesecake in a bowl and blend until very creamy. Stir in the dissolved and cooled gelatine and then fold in the egg whites. Spoon the mixture over the base and smooth over. Chill in the deep freeze for 15 minutes and then transfer to the refrigerator and leave until firmly set.

Meanwhile, make your chosen sauce and topping. For the Chocolate or Carob Fudge Sauce and banana topping, prepare the sauce and decorate the cheesecake in concentric circles with the sliced banana. Serve the cheesecake with the warm sauce. For the fruit sauce and topping, reserve some of the berries for decoration and process the remainder in a blender along with the rosewater and enough cold filtered water to give the desired consistency. Sieve if necessary. Melt the jam (jelly) in a small pan, brush over the reserved fruit, leave to set in the refrigerator and then use to decorate the cheesecake. Serve accompanied by the fruit sauce.

Bramble Fool

Blackberries are high in vitamin C and folic acid and blend well with raspberries and strawberries. As blackberries are not in season when the other fruits are, I use frozen blackberries. In the autumn (fall) of course, you can use fresh wild blackberries and frozen raspberries and strawberries. Soft fruits go mouldy quickly, so check them carefully before you buy and don't wash them until needed.

Makes about 8 servings

550g/3 cups mixed soft organic fruits – blackberries, raspberries and strawberries (frozen or fresh but at least one red fruit and one black fruit)
100g/½ cup unrefined caster (superfine) sugar
Finely grated rind and juice of ½ an unwaxed organic lemon
11.7g/1½ tablespoons gelatine or the vegetarian equivalent
250ml/1 cup coconut cream or organic coconut milk
250ml/1 cup soya cream
115g/⅔ cup fresh organic berries of your choice for decoration

Put the soft fruit in a saucepan with the sugar, lemon rind and juice. Cook for a few minutes until just soft. Remove from the heat, stir in the gelatine granules, allow to cool, stirring occasionally, then liquidize in a blender or food processor.

Sieve the mixture into a bowl, discarding any pips and stalks. When the mixture is cold, chill it in the refrigerator until it begins to set then quickly stir in the coconut cream and soya cream. Spoon the mixture into a glass bowl and gently smooth over. Cover and chill in the refrigerator until set.

Decorate with some fresh berries and serve the fool chilled.

Chocolate or Carob Fudge Sauce

This irresistible sauce is quick and easy to make and is delicious with dairy-free vanilla, butterscotch or chocolate ice creams. It is also excellent drizzled over baked bananas or pears. You can keep it in a sealed container in the fridge for about a week and simply heat it through in a small non-stick pan whenever you need some.

If your child cannot eat chocolate, make the sauce with carob – just stir in 2 tablespoons of carob powder instead of the cocoa.

GF   WF   DF   EF   NF   YF   V

Makes about 8 servings

55g/2oz dairy-free margarine
140g/¾ cup unrefined dark soft brown sugar
140g/½ cup golden syrup (corn syrup)
125ml/½ cup soya cream
2 heaped tablespoons organic dairy-free cocoa powder*
½ teaspoon pure vanilla extract

* coeliacs please use gluten-free ingredients

Put the margarine, sugar and syrup into a pan and melt over medium heat. Increase the heat to high and bring the sauce to the boil, cook for about 3 minutes and remove from the heat.

Once the bubbling has subsided, stir in the cream, cocoa and vanilla, return to the heat and simmer at bubbling point for a further 5 minutes. Remove from the heat and serve warm. Each time you reheat the sauce at a high temperature for a few minutes, it will thicken up and become more fudge like.

 Cold desserts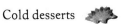

Little Fruit Yogurt Pots

If everyone around you is feeding their toddlers and children on mini yogurts and fromage frais then it is very frustrating that nothing similar is available for lactose-intolerant children. This is a good little trick but not for children less than 2 years of age. You can buy soya junior yogurts but they come in standard-size packs.

Makes 6

GF　WF　DF　EF　NF　YF　V

250g/1 cup soya yogurt (Provamel Yofu junior fruit or organic natural)
24 ripe organic raspberries, or tiny pieces of other suitable soft and ripe fruit (apricot, peach or mango)
1 × 6 pack of mini-size yogurt or fromage frais (i.e. Petits Filous)

When you or your other children have finished eating their mini yogurts, take the pack and the peel-back lids and wash in very hot water with your usual germ-killing washing up liquid. Rinse and wipe clean with absorbent kitchen paper. Try to keep the labels dry and lids intact whilst doing this.

Put the yogurt into a bowl, mix and crush in the raspberries. Carefully three-quarters fill the clean and dry pots with the mixture and smooth over. Wipe away any dribbles, cover with the lids and chill until needed. Eat on the day of making.

Hot desserts

Blueberry Pancakes with Raspberry Sauce

Do not be tempted to replace the buckwheat with more gluten-free flour mix as it will be too thick; you can however replace the gluten-free flour with rice flour. You can also use any mixture of fruit – try sliced banana with apricot sauce, peach with blackberry sauce, or cooked apple or pear with raspberry sauce. Get the kids to make their own pancakes – the idea is for them to have more fruit, less pancakes and no sugar, so get them to pile the fruit high and cover the pancakes with lashings of sauce. If you wish, provide a selection of fruit fillings in bowls so that the kids can have fun picking and mixing.

OPTIONAL

Serves 4–8

GF   WF   DF   NF   V   EF

Sauce and filling (the smaller amount serves 4–6, the larger amount 8)

340–500g/generous 2–3 cups fresh organic raspberries

A dash of pure rosewater

250g–375g/generous 2–3 cups fresh organic blueberries (or other peeled and thinly sliced organic fruits such as blackberries, peaches and apricots, or cooked and unsweetened fruits such as apple or pear)

Pancakes (makes about 16)

55g/scant ½ cup gluten-free flour mix

55g/scant ½ cup organic buckwheat flour

A pinch of fine salt (optional)

3 large organic free-range eggs or 3 heaped teaspoons of Orgran No Egg egg replacer and 6 tablespoons cold filtered water

250ml/1 cup soya or rice milk (goat's or sheep's milk is fine if not on a dairy-free diet)

2 tablespoons warm melted dairy-free margarine

A little cold pressed sunflower oil, for frying

18cm/7in griddle or a non-stick frying pan (skillet)

A little extra oil for frying

16 squares (roughly the same size as the pancakes) of baking parchment (wax paper) for stacking the pancakes

First make the sauce by blending the raspberries with the dash of rosewater and enough cold filtered water to produce a purée of pouring consistency. Sieve to remove pips and transfer the sauce to a jug.

To make the pancakes with eggs: Mix the first three ingredients together in a bowl, make a well in the centre and whisk in the eggs until thoroughly incorporated. Gradually whisk in the milk and the melted margarine until the batter is smooth. Transfer to a pouring jug and leave for 20–30 minutes before using.

To make the pancakes without eggs: Mix together the first three ingredients in a bowl, stir in the egg replacer and then gradually whisk in the measured water for the egg replacer, the milk and the melted margarine. Whisk until you have a smooth batter, transfer to a pouring jug and leave for 20–30 minutes before using. You will probably have to increase the amount of milk you use according to the absorbency of the gluten-free flour. Whisk in a little at a time until you have an easily pourable mixture.

To cook the pancakes, pour a little of the batter onto a hot, lightly oiled frying pan (skillet), swirling and tilting the pan around so that the surface is completely covered with a very thin layer of the batter. Turn the pancake when bubbles form on the surface and it is golden brown underneath. If it is too pale it will be soggy. Flip it over and cook on the other side until golden brown. Carefully slide the pancake onto a layer of parchment (wax paper) on a warm plate. Repeat the process until all the batter is used up and you have a stack of pancakes, each one separated by parchment (wax paper) to prevent them from sticking to each other.

Have warm plates ready and quickly place a couple of pancakes on each plate, pour over the sauce, add a pile of berries and serve immediately.

Alternatively, if you wish to serve the pancakes as finger food, you can spread a thin layer of sauce over the inside of each pancake, sprinkle with some berries, roll up and serve immediately.

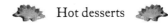

Apple and Almond Butterscotch Tart

If nuts are to be avoided then you can top this tart with a thick sprinkling of brown sugar instead. We often have this dessert for Sunday lunch in the autumn (fall) when our apples have fallen off the tree and are scattered all over the grass.

OPTIONAL

GF   WF   DF   YF   V   EF   NF

Makes one 25cm/10in tart

Pastry

255g/2 generous cups gluten-free flour mix

130g/4½oz dairy-free margarine and a little extra for greasing

1 tablespoon pure orange water (and a little cold water if not using egg)

Optional – 1 organic free-range egg if not on an egg-free diet

Filling and topping

800g/1lb 12oz organic eating apples, peeled, cored and cut into eights

Juice of ½ a large unwaxed organic lemon

A sprinkling of ground cloves

150g/1 scant cup light muscovado sugar

4 tablespoons gluten-free flour mix

4 tablespoons soya cream

2 heaped teaspoons Orgran No Egg egg replacer and 4 tablespoons of water or 2 organic free-range eggs

Optional – 100g/3½oz pack flaked almonds if not on a nut-free diet or use a thick sprinkling of demerara
   sugar

25.5cm/10in fluted tart tin or quiche dish, greased and floured*

Non-stick baking parchment (wax paper) and ceramic baking beans

* coeliacs please use gluten-free ingredients

Preheat the oven to 180°C/350°F/Gas mark 4.

Make the pastry by mixing the flour and margarine in a food processor until it resembles breadcrumbs. Add the orange water and the egg, and blend briefly until it comes together into a dough. If not using egg then just add the orange water followed by a little cold filtered water at a time until the mixture comes together into a dough. (The amount of water also depends on the flour used.) Wrap the dough in clingfilm (plastic wrap) and chill for 30 minutes.

Meanwhile, put the prepared apples into a pan and simmer with a little water – just enough to prevent them from sticking to the bottom of the pan. Sprinkle with the lemon juice to prevent them going brown and add the cloves. As soon as the apples are just about soft, take them off the heat and leave to cool.

Roll out the pastry on a floured board and line the prepared tart tin. Let the pastry hang over the edge and then crimp it between your fingers so that you have a good solid edge and the pastry will not shrink back. Prick the base of the pastry with a sharp knife or with a fork. Line the pastry with a circle of non-stick baking parchment (wax paper) and some ceramic beans. Bake the pastry blind for about 15 minutes or until pale gold; remove from the oven, carefully lift out the paper with the beans and set aside to cool. Return the pastry to the oven and cook for 5 minutes to crisp up the base. Take out of the oven and leave to cool.

In a small bowl, mix the sugar with the flour and cream and stir in the eggs, if using, until smooth. Alternatively, add the egg replacer to the sugar, flour and cream mixture and stir in the 4 tablespoons of water.

Assemble the pudding quickly. Fill the pastry with the apples, leaving any juices behind so that the pastry will not become soggy, spread the sugar and cream mixture all over the apples and sprinkle with the almonds or sugar. Bake the tart in the centre of the oven for about 35 minutes until just firm and golden, making sure that the nuts do not become burnt.

Serve the pudding warm with some dairy-free vanilla ice cream.

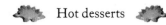 Hot desserts

Castle Puddings

We used to have such fun making these as children and I very much hope that you will teach your children to make them too. With any luck some of the mixture will end up in the moulds! You can vary this recipe by serving the puddings with warmed golden (corn) syrup instead of jam (jelly).

OPTIONAL

GF   WF   DF   NF   YF   V   EF

Makes 4

85g/3oz dairy-free margarine

85g/scant ½ cup vanilla caster (superfine) sugar

The contents of 1 vanilla pod or 1 teaspoon pure vanilla extract

2 heaped teaspoons Orgran No Egg egg replacer and 4 tablespoons of cold water (or 2 large organic free-
    range eggs if not on an egg-free diet)

150g/1 heaped cup gluten-free flour mix, sifted

1 teaspoon gluten-free baking powder

About 2 tablespoons allergy-free milk to mix (depending on flour absorbency)

4 tablespoons sugar-free raspberry jam (jelly)

4 large tin pudding moulds or 4 large ramekins, bases lined with a circle of non-stick baking parchment (wax
    paper) and sides lightly greased with dairy-free margarine and dusted with gluten-free flour

Preheat the oven to 180°C/350°F/Gas Mark 4.

Place the margarine, sugar and vanilla in a large mixing bowl and beat them together, using a wooden spoon, until soft and pale. Beat in one egg at a time, if using, while alternately and lightly mixing in the flour. Now very briefly mix in the baking powder and lastly, and equally briefly, mix in the milk. Alternatively, mix everything together in a food processor. If you are not using eggs, briefly mix the egg replacer and measured water into the creamed margarine, very briefly mix in the flour and baking powder and lastly, and just as briefly, mix in the milk.

Don't fill the moulds right to the top otherwise they will be too big for smaller children or they may overflow – instead aim for about three-quarters full. Flatten the top of the mixture to ensure that the puddings sit firmly on the plates when they are turned out. If they rise too much and are too rounded you can slice the tops off and discard them. If you use egg replacer rather than fresh egg, the puddings don't rise quite as much so they should end up fairly level. Place the moulds on a baking tray and bake for about 35 minutes until well risen and golden.

Meanwhile, gently heat the raspberry jam (jelly) in a small pan until warm and runny. Take the tray of puddings out of the oven and let them cool for 5 minutes. Hold one at a time firmly in a thick dry cloth or with oven gloves and, with the help of a palette knife, turn each one out onto warm plates. Don't forget that you can slice off the top if the castles are too wobbly! Pour over some warm raspberry jam (jelly) and serve immediately.

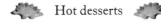

Steamed Blueberry Pudding

As we are aiming to get kids to eat between five and seven portions of fruit and vegetables a day, we have to try to sneak as many as we can into a meal. This pudding has masses of sweet and juicy blueberries and should be tempting enough for the most fruit-shy child.

OPTIONAL

GF   WF   DF   NF   YF   V   EF

Serves about 6

500g/1¼lb ripe blueberries or bag of frozen and nearly defrosted mixed summer berries

A pinch of ground cinnamon

130g/¾ cup unrefined caster (superfine) sugar

130g/4½oz softened dairy-free margarine plus a little extra for greasing

2 heaped teaspoons Orgran No Egg egg replacer and 4 tablespoons of cold water (or 2 organic free-range eggs if not on an egg-free diet)

130g/1 heaped cup gluten-free flour mix, sifted into a dish with 1 heaped teaspoon gluten-free baking powder

2 litre/4½ pint (US) heatproof pudding basin, greased and floured

String, non-stick baking parchment (wax paper) and foil

Put the berries and cinnamon in a pan and place over a gentle heat until the fruit begins to release its juices – remove from the heat before they begin to stew.

If using defrosted fruits, discard excess juices or the pudding will be soggy. Set aside.

Beat the sugar and margarine thoroughly until pale and light, then add the eggs one at a time and blend thoroughly. (This can be done in a food processor by grown ups or in a mixing bowl with a wooden spoon by children.) Add the flour and baking powder to the mixture and gently stir them in, along with the vanilla. For the egg-free recipe, beat the sugar and margarine together and then add the flour, baking powder and vanilla. Sprinkle over the egg replacer and lastly add the water and mix briefly. If you are using a food processor then spoon the prepared pudding mixture into a bowl before continuing with the recipe.

Pour the fruit over the top of the pudding mixture and fold in gently. Using a spatula, scrape the mixture into the prepared pudding basin and gently level off the top. Cover the basin with a double sheet of pleated non-stick baking parchment (wax paper), secure with string and cover tightly with foil. If it is a plastic basin it may have a lid, which you can reuse. Steam the pudding for 2 hours in a large pan of boiling water – the water should come halfway up the sides of the basin. From time to time check and add more water if it is getting low.

Carefully lift the pudding basin out of the simmering water and leave to cool for about 5 minutes. Remove the foil, string and parchment (wax paper) and turn out on to a warm plate. Serve the pudding warm.

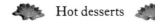

Upside Down Pineapple Ginger Pudding

This is a lovely warming winter pudding and ideal for Sunday lunch – as long as you follow it with a hearty walk or some games in the garden to work off the sugar and fat. Fresh ginger has so many wonderful properties and children love the flavour, as we can see from the popularity of gingerbread cakes and cookies.

Makes about 8 servings

Sponge

115g/4oz very soft dairy-free margarine

3 heaped teaspoons Orgran No Egg egg replacer and 6 tablespoons filtered hot water (or 3 organic free-range eggs if not on an egg-free diet)

4 heaped tablespoons organic blackstrap molasses

225g/2 cups gluten-free flour mix

½ teaspoon each ground cinnamon and freshly grated nutmeg

¼ teaspoon ground cloves

2 heaped teaspoons finely grated organic root ginger

80ml/⅓ cup of the liquid from the canned organic pineapple slices (or more depending on absorbency of flour)

2 large organic sweet apples, peeled and grated

2 teaspoons gluten-free baking powder

Topping

55g/2oz dairy-free softened margarine

55g/⅓ cup unrefined brown sugar

425g/15oz can sliced organic pineapple (packed in juice not syrup), drained

25.5 cm/10in round, deep cake tin

Preheat the oven to 180°C/350°F/Gas mark 4.

In a mixing bowl, beat the margarine with the molasses and then beat in a little hot water at a time until smooth. Now fold in the flour, egg replacer and the 6 tablespoons of water, one at a time, until smooth. If you are using eggs, mix the margarine, eggs and molasses together in a mixing bowl with a metal whisk and then beat in the flour until smooth.

Lightly fold in the spices and grated ginger. Stir the pineapple liquid and grated apple into the mixture and briefly fold in the baking powder.

Spread the margarine for the topping over the bottom and halfway up the sides of the cake tin. Sprinkle the brown sugar over the margarine and place the sliced pineapple attractively over the sugar. Pour in the cake mix and bake for 40–50 minutes until the sponge is cooked through.

Once out of the oven immediately and carefully invert onto a warm serving plate – wear heatproof gloves or use a cloth. Any fruit that sticks to the pan can be carefully placed back on the pudding using a non-stick palette knife or spatula.

Serve the pudding warm; it is delicious with dairy-free vanilla ice cream.

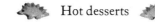

Hot Chocolate Fudge Magic Pudding

This is rather like a chocolate pond pudding where, on cutting, chocolate oozes out. It is perfect for children of all ages and my goddaughter Charlotte and her brother William love making this for special occasions such as their mother's birthday.

OPTIONAL

GF   WF   DF   NF   YF   V   EF

Makes about 8 servings

100g/⅔ cup gluten-free flour mix

1 heaped teaspoon gluten-free baking powder

5 tablespoons organic dairy-free cocoa powder*

A pinch of fine salt (optional)

55g/2oz dairy- and nut-free chocolate chips, drops or pieces*

115g/4oz dairy-free margarine

115g/½ cup plus 1 tablespoon caster (superfine) sugar

2 heaped teaspoons Orgran No Egg egg replacer and 6 tablespoons of cold filtered water or 2 large organic free-range eggs

1 teaspoon pure vanilla extract

115g/½ cup plus 1 tablespoon unrefined soft brown sugar

320ml/1⅓ cups boiling filtered water

23cm/9in square or oval ovenproof dish, lightly greased

* coeliacs please use gluten-free ingredients

Preheat the oven to 180°C/350°F/Gas mark 5.

Sift the flour, baking powder, 1 tablespoon of the cocoa powder and the salt, if using, into a bowl and then fold in the chocolate chips.

In another large bowl, beat the margarine and sugar until pale and light with a wooden spoon or beat in the food processor. Briefly beat in the eggs, if using, and then the vanilla or briefly beat in the egg replacer and measured water with the vanilla. Now mix in the sifted dry ingredients. Spoon the mixture into the prepared dish and gently level off.

Mix the brown sugar with the remaining cocoa and the boiling water in a bowl and pour it all over the cake mixture. Bake the pudding for about 30 minutes or until the sponge is just firm and the sauce has sunk to the bottom.

Serve the pudding as soon as possible so that the sauce doesn't get absorbed into the sponge. It is delicious served warm with a dollop of vanilla dairy-free ice cream.

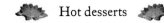 Hot desserts

Baking

Animal Cookies

There are so many fun cookie cutters available – animals are always popular so there are usually plenty to choose from. Stars and Christmas trees are great for a bit of festive spirit and gingerbread men cutters can be made into instant snowmen with a touch of white icing and lots of coloured icing for a scarf, face and hat. These cookies are very plain and simple so they are ideal for 2–3 year olds. You could omit the vanilla and use finely grated lemon zest instead.

Makes about 16

2 teaspoons arrowroot powder

300g/2½ cups gluten-free flour mix

½ teaspoon gluten-free baking powder

185g/6½oz dairy-free margarine

130g/¾ cup unrefined caster (superfine) sugar

1½ teaspoons pure vanilla extract

1 heaped teaspoon gluten-free baking powder mixed with 1½ tablespoons cold pressed sunflower oil and
  1½ tablespoons water

Optional – suitable ready-made coloured icing* and other decorations* to embellish your animals, stars,
  Christmas trees or figures. Please check the labels to make sure that the ingredients are allergy-free for the
  children eating them

* coeliacs please use gluten-free ingredients

 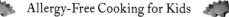

Preheat oven to 190°C/375°F/Gas mark 5.

Mix the arrowroot, flour and baking powder in a bowl and set aside. Cream the margarine, sugar and vanilla together in another bowl. Beat the baking powder, oil and water mixture into the margarine and gradually blend in the flour mixture.

Bring the dough together into a ball with your hands, flatten and divide into quarters. Roll one piece out thickly on a clean and floured board with a floured rolling pin. Cut out your favourite animal shapes and carefully transfer them onto ungreased non-stick baking trays. Bake them in the centre of the oven for about 8 minutes. Remove the trays from the oven and leave the cookies on the baking trays for a few minutes before transferring to wire racks.

When the cookies are cold you can decorate them with piped coloured icing and other allergy-free and fun decorations. As even more of a treat you can make chocolate animals – add 55g/2oz melted dairy- and nut-free dark chocolate* to the mixture and ¼ teaspoon of gluten-free bicarbonate of soda (baking soda) instead of the ½ teaspoon of baking powder. If your child cannot eat chocolate, use a chopped up dairy- and nut-free carob bar instead.

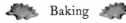

Baking

Carob Chip and Brazil Nut Cookies

These cookies are brilliant bribery for children of all ages! You can change the carob pieces or flakes for real dark chocolate chips if suitable and you can vary the nuts by using organic whole almonds. For a nut-free version, use chopped unsulphured dried apricots or other fruit or berries with seeds.

Makes 18

125g/1 heaped cup gluten-free flour mix
½ teaspoon gluten-free bicarbonate of soda (baking soda)
55g/¼ cup unrefined soft brown sugar
55g/¼ cup vanilla sugar (or add 1 teaspoon vanilla extract to unrefined cane sugar)
70g/2½oz dairy-free margarine
1 large organic free-range egg
55g/⅓ cup finely chopped organic Brazil nuts
100g/3½oz dairy-free chocolate-style carob bar*, chopped into small pieces or carob flakes* or carob chips*
   (see page 192 for brands and stockists)

3 greased baking sheets

* coeliacs please use gluten-free ingredients

Preheat the oven to 180°C/350°F/Gas mark 4.

Combine the first six ingredients in a food processor and whiz until blended. Add the nuts and carob pieces and mix briefly. Spoon small mounds of the mixture onto the greased baking sheets and keep them well spaced out. Bake the cookies for 7–10 minutes until golden brown. Leave for 2 minutes then lift them off and place them on a wire rack to cool.

Carob Apples on Sticks

Rather than caramel-, toffee- or chocolate-coated apples at Halloween or fireworks parties, why not try this healthier version. Make them fun by letting the kids decorate the apples themselves.

OPTIONAL

GF WF DF EF YF V NF

Makes 6–8

450g/3 cups icing (confectioners) sugar, sifted
70g/½ cup carob powder
1 teaspoon pure vanilla extract
Boiling filtered water
Flat, wooden lollypop (craft) sticks
Unbruised organic eating apples, stalk removed

For decoration
Allergy-free mini marshmallows, carob bar shavings or drops, coconut flakes (if not on a nut-free diet), or
   other allowed candy pieces

In a bowl, mix the sugar, carob powder and vanilla. Add a little boiling water at a time and beat the mixture until it becomes a spreadable consistency. Set aside.

Insert the sticks into the bottoms of the apples. Spread and swirl the top half of each apple with some of the mixture until well coated. Decorate and then place them on non-stick baking parchment (wax paper) and refrigerate until ready to eat.

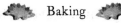

Lemon and Pine Nut Tarts

These little Italian tarts are made with pine nuts, which are sometimes classified as seeds not nuts. However, for safety reasons, in this book they have been classified as nuts. Tarts similar to these are served in Italy with steaming cups of cappuccino and other tempting petits fours. This recipe should appeal to children of all ages – so the chef will be able to enjoy the treat too!

Makes 30

Pastry

130g/4½oz dairy-free margarine
255g/2 generous cups gluten-free flour
Finely grated rind of ½ an unwaxed organic lemon
1 large organic free-range egg, lightly beaten
A little cold filtered water

Filling

2 large organic free-range eggs
60g/⅓ cup caster (superfine) sugar
Finely grated rind of 1½ unwaxed organic lemons
3 tablespoons freshly squeezed lemon juice
2 tablespoons toasted organic pine nuts, grilled (broiled) until golden

12-bun non-stick tart or muffin tin, lightly greased
12 circles of non-stick baking parchment (wax paper) to line the tin
Ceramic baking beans
9cm/3½in-round fluted pastry cutter

Preheat the oven to 200°C/400°F/Gas mark 6.

Mix the margarine with the flour in a food processor until it resembles fine breadcrumbs. Add the grated lemon rind and the egg to the mixture and whiz again until it comes together into a ball of dough. You may need a little cold water to do this, depending on which kind of flour you have used. Remove the pastry from the processor, wrap in clingfilm (plastic wrap) and chill for about 30 minutes.

Roll out the dough thinly and cut out circles with the fluted cutter – you will need to roll the offcuts to make the 12 circles. Carefully line the tin with the pastry circles, then line each tart with a small circle of non-stick paper and some ceramic beans. Bake the pastry blind for about 8 minutes or until the tarts are pale golden brown. Carefully remove the paper and beans.

Make the filling by beating the eggs with the sugar, lemon rind and juice. Pour the filling into the pastry cases and top each one with some pine nuts. Bake the tarts for another 10 minutes or until the filling is firm and the pastry golden. Remove from the oven and cool on a wire rack before serving.

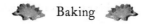

Airy Fairy Cakes

These cakes are as light as clouds inside and slightly chewy on the outside, something that all the tiny tots that tried them loved. They need to be eaten fresh on the day of baking. Decorate them to suit any occasion or season. You can make 24 mini cakes for parties.

OPTIONAL

GF   WF   DF   NF   YF   V   EF

Makes 12

Cakes

125g/1 heaped cup gluten-free flour mix

115g/4oz very soft dairy-free margarine (Pure is good)

115g/⅔ cup unrefined caster (superfine) sugar

2 heaped teaspoons Orgran No Egg egg replacer and 4 tablespoons of cold water or 2 organic free-range eggs if not on an egg-free diet

2 teaspoons pure vanilla extract or the same amount of fresh lemon, lime or orange juice

2 teaspoons gluten-free baking powder

2 tablespoons organic unsweetened soya milk (or rice, almond or oat depending on diet); the absorbency of flours varies so you may need more

Icing

About 200g/¾ cup icing (confectioners) sugar, sifted

1 teaspoon pure vanilla extract or a few drops of Boyajian lemon, lime or orange oils (see page 197 for stockist)

12 natural-coloured glacé cherries

12-cup, non-stick deep bun tray lined with 12 circles on non-stick baking parchment (wax paper) or 12 large non-stick paper cases

Preheat the oven to 190°C/375°F/Gas mark 5.

If you are using fresh eggs, put all the cake ingredients in the food processor except the milk. Blend the ingredients briefly, add the milk and blend briefly until smooth.

If you are using egg replacer, put the flour, margarine, sugar, vanilla, baking powder and egg replacer in the food processor. Add the milk and then the 4 tablespoons of water and blend briefly until smooth.

Divide the mixture between the paper cases and bake for about 25 minutes until pale golden brown and well risen. Remove from the oven and leave to cool. Transfer them to a wire rack as soon as you can handle them.

When the cakes are cold, mix the icing (confectioners) sugar in a bowl with your chosen flavouring and a little cold filtered water until you can spread the icing evenly and smoothly over each fairy cake. Top each one with a cherry and serve.

I also use brilliant dairy-, sugar- and gluten-free Christmas and Easter chocolate and carob decorations, which can bought by mail order (see page 194).

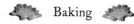

Mini Chocolate Muffins

Anything made with chocolate is always a great hit in our family. These are not only ideal for parties but for freezing and popping into school lunch boxes.

OPTIONAL

GF WF DF NF YF V EF

Makes 24

Muffins

150g/1 heaped cup gluten-free flour mix

2 tablespoons organic dairy-free cocoa powder*

1 dessertspoon gluten-free baking powder

A pinch of fine salt (optional)

55g/2 × 1oz squares of dairy- and nut-free dark chocolate* (at least 70 per cent cocoa solids), roughly chopped into small pieces

1 large egg or 1 heaped teaspoon of Orgran No Egg egg replacer and 2 tablespoons of filtered cold water

40g/scant ¼ cup unrefined caster (superfine) sugar

125ml/½ cup organic unsweetened soya milk (or rice, oat or almond milk depending on diet)

55g/2oz dairy-free margarine, melted and cooled slightly

Topping

100g/3½ × 1oz squares dairy- and nut-free dark chocolate* (at least 70 per cent cocoa solids), broken into pieces

1 teaspoon cold pressed sunflower oil

1 tablespoon organic sunflower seeds

2 × 12-bun mini tart/muffin tins, well greased or lined with mini-muffin non-stick paper cases

* coeliacs please use gluten-free ingredients

Preheat the oven to 200°C/400°F/Gas mark 6.

Sift the flour, cocoa powder, baking powder and salt, if using, into a large bowl and mix together with the chocolate pieces. If you are using the egg replacer, add it to the dry ingredients. Then, in a separate bowl, mix together the egg or the measured water for the egg replacer, sugar, milk and melted margarine. Quickly fold the wet mixture into the dry mixture using a large metal spoon.

Place about 1 heaped teaspoon of the mixture in each of the muffin cups and bake in the oven for 8–10 minutes until spongy and firm to touch. Remove the muffins from the oven and cool in the tins for 5 minutes before transferring them to a wire rack.

While the muffins are cooling, make the topping. Place the broken up chocolate in a small heatproof bowl, over a saucepan of barely simmering water. Slowly melt the chocolate, add the oil and stir until glossy. Cool for 2–3 minutes and when the muffins are cool enough to handle, spread a little melted chocolate on top of each one. Place each one back on the wire rack and scatter the sunflower seeds over the top of each muffin.

For Easter, you can decorate each muffin with some Whizzers speckled eggs (see page 194 for stockist) or other nut-free brands.

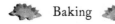

Sugar-Free Almond Brownies

I have exchanged the standard pecans for whole almonds in this recipe because almonds tend to be less problematic than other nuts and they are an excellent source of protein and calcium. This is particularly helpful to kids on a dairy-free diet who will probably be eating less calcium. As these brownies are sugar-free, they are a much healthier snack for the lunchbox or at teatime.

Makes 16 small squares or 8 fingers

30g/1oz dairy-free margarine
85g/3 × 1oz squares unsweetened dairy-free chocolate* (at least 70 per cent cocoa solids)
125ml/½ cup malted brown rice syrup (see brand and stockist page 192)
2 large organic free-range eggs
1 teaspoon pure vanilla extract
70g/½ cup gluten-free flour mix
70g/½ cup organic skinned almonds, sliced in half
Optional – sugar- and dairy-free cocoa powder* for dusting or 1 bar of sugar- and dairy-free chocolate*, melted with a few drops of oil and beaten until glossy

20 × 20cm/8 × 8in baking pan, greased with a little dairy-free margarine

* coeliacs please use gluten-free ingredients

Preheat the oven to 180°C/350°F/Gas mark 4.

Melt the margarine and chocolate in a medium-sized pan over low heat. Stir in the brown rice syrup and remove the mixture from the heat. Stir in the eggs one at a time, add the vanilla and then stir in the flour and nuts.

Transfer the mixture to the prepared tin and gently spread it out and level it off. Bake for 25–30 minutes until just set. Cool the brownies and then cut into squares or fingers.

For older kids, you can lightly dust the brownies with cocoa powder or spread them with the melted chocolate and chill until set. For a double whammy, spread with the chocolate and then dust with cocoa!

In the unlikely event that there are any left, store them in an airtight container.

 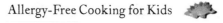

Cherry Muffins

Muffins are easy fillers for the lunchbox and you can vary them by substituting ready-to-eat dried cranberries for the cherries. Keep any leftover muffins in a sealed container for the next day – you can drizzle some lemon icing over them and take them on a picnic.

Makes 8

115g/1 cup gluten-free flour mix
70g/½ cup fine organic oatmeal or bran
1 teaspoon gluten-free bicarbonate of soda (baking soda)
1 teaspoon gluten-free cream of tartar
40g/⅓ cup ready-to eat dried cherries
200g/¾ cup applesauce*
60ml/¼ cup prune juice
1 tablespoon cold pressed sunflower oil

12-cup muffin tin lined with 8 non-stick paper muffin cases

* coeliacs please use gluten-free ingredients

Preheat the oven to 200°C/400°F/Gas mark 6.

Combine the first four ingredients in a mixing bowl and then stir in the cherries.

Using a separate bowl, mix together the applesauce, prune juice and oil. Add the wet ingredients to the dry ingredients and mix well.

Spoon the mixture into the paper cases and bake for about 17–20 minutes until firm and springy to touch. When they are cool enough to handle, transfer them to a wire rack to cool. They are delicious eaten warm.

Mini Mince Pies

This mincemeat is colourful and the extra vitamin C from the cranberries will help keep everyone going at full steam over Christmas! You can make the mince pies in advance and freeze them.

This recipe makes about 36 tiny pies but the mincemeat is enough for you to double up the pastry recipe and knock out 72 for a party. Otherwise, seal the leftover mincemeat in sterilized jars and store in the refrigerator for your next batch. Bring the mincemeat back to a warm room temperature and add a little more orange juice and brandy if it seems dry.

Makes 36

Mincemeat
75g/¾ cup fresh cranberries
100g/1 cup organic sultanas (golden raisins)
150g/1¼ cups organic raisins
60g/⅔ cup organic currants
100g/¾ cup organic mixed dried peel
75g/½ cup dried cranberries
150g/¾ cup unrefined cane sugar (use a bit more if you all have a sweet tooth)
80g/¾ cup dairy-free and gluten-free Broadlands vegetable suet (see page 196)
1 teaspoon allspice
1 teaspoon cinnamon
½ teaspoon freshly grated nutmeg
Finely grated rind of 1 unwaxed organic lemon
1 organic eating apple, washed, cored and grated
Finely grated rind and juice of 1 unwaxed organic orange
60ml/¼ cup good brandy (if on a yeast-free diet use a fruit juice) or, if you prefer no alcohol, use apple juice

Pastry
255g/2 generous cups gluten-free flour mix
55g/2oz dairy-free margarine
55g/2oz vegetable shortening (Cookeen is good)
Optional – 1 organic free-range egg
1 tablespoon pure rosewater
A little cold filtered water if not using an egg

Cinnamon sugar
½ teaspoon ground cinnamon mixed with 1 tablespoon unrefined caster (superfine) sugar

2 x 12-bun non-stick baking tins or mince pie tins
5cm/2in round fluted cutter and a very small star-shaped cutter

---

Make the mincemeat first. Blend all but the last two mincemeat ingredients in a bowl and then moisten with the orange juice and brandy, apple or fruit juice. Cover and keep in a cold place overnight. Transfer the mixture into an ovenproof dish, cover with foil and bake for about 1½ hours in the oven at 140°C/275°F/Gas mark 1.

Meanwhile, make the pastry. Briefly combine the flour, margarine and shortening in a food processor until the mixture resembles breadcrumbs. With the machine running, add the egg, if using, and then the rosewater. If you are not using an egg, then add the rosewater and then just enough water for the dough to come together in a ball. Scrape the pastry out of the bowl and onto a floured board or clean surface. Wrap the pastry in clingfilm (plastic wrap) and chill for about 30 minutes. Turn the oven temperature up to 190°C/375°F/Gas mark 5.

Unwrap the pastry and thinly roll it out on a floured board or a clean and floured surface. Cut as many rounds as you can with the pastry cutter and the same again with the star-shaped cutter.

Line the tins with the pastry circles and push down gently. Fill each with a tiny spoonful of mincemeat and cover with a star-shaped pastry top. Sprinkle with the cinnamon sugar and bake for about 25 minutes until the pastry is golden and the mincemeat is bubbling.

 Baking

Yule Log

Cocoa contains iron and is a source of magnesium, which is used for a wide variety of body functions, including building bones. So this traditional Yule log has some benefits, as well as being festive and fun for children at Christmas.

Serves 12 or more

GF **WF** **DF** **NF** **YF** **V**

Roulade

5 large organic free-range eggs, separated

170g/1 cup unrefined caster sugar

140g/5 × 1oz squares of dairy- and nut-free dark chocolate* (at least 70 per cent cocoa solids)

3 tablespoons cold filtered water

½ teaspoon pure vanilla extract

Icing and decorations

255g/9oz dairy-free margarine

340g/12oz icing (confectioners) sugar, sieved until smooth and fine

4 tablespoons organic dairy-free cocoa powder*

60ml/¼ cup warm filtered water

Christmas decorations made from plastic or icing sugar but not marzipan if on a nut-free diet – you can usually find reindeer, robins, holly and Father Christmas in kitchen stores or superstores

30.5 × 38cm/11 × 14in non-stick Swiss roll/roulade tin lined with non-stick baking parchment (wax paper), plus a spare sheet

* coeliacs please use gluten-free ingredients

Preheat the oven to 180°C/350°F/Gas mark 4.

Beat the egg yolks in a bowl with the sugar until pale and fluffy. Melt the chocolate in a bowl set over boiling water or in the microwave. Stir the chocolate into the egg yolks. Add the cold water and vanilla extract.

Whisk the egg whites until stiff and then fold into the chocolate mixture. Spread the mixture over the prepared tray and bake until firm and spongy, about 15 minutes. Set the roulade tin on a wire rack and cover with a clean damp cloth until cold. Remove the cloth and loosen the paper from around the edges. Dust another sheet of non-stick paper with a little extra sieved icing (confectioners) sugar and turn the roulade onto it. Peel off the paper and discard it.

Make the icing in a food processor by whizzing up the margarine, icing (confectioners) sugar, cocoa and water until smooth. Spread the surface of the roulade with about ⅓ of the mixture and then carefully, and using the paper to guide you, roll up the roulade. Lift the roulade onto a serving plate and discard the paper.

Cut a piece off the end of the roulade about 7.5cm/3in long and move it to a jaunty angle against the side of the 'log'. This will now look more log-like! Cover the entire log with the remaining icing. Run fork prongs along the icing to make log-like furrows in the bark. Dust the Yule log with sieved icing (confectioners) sugar and decorate with anything you fancy. Please make sure you use safe decorations that cannot harm your children. Cover and chill the Yule log until needed.

If you keep the Yule log sealed under clingfilm (plastic wrap), it will keep in the refrigerator for up to a week.

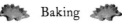

Christmas Cake

As nut-free diets are particularly difficult at Christmas, my mince pies, Yule log, stuffed turkey and Christmas cake are all nut free. I have given you some alternative icings and decorations for this cake, so it can also be used as a special occasion or weekend cake throughout the year.

The cake is very low in fat if you use the egg-whites-only recipe and the dried fruit is a concentrated source of essential minerals, including iron. The sweetness of dried fruit comes from the natural sugar or fructose it contains, so this is a healthy treat for picnics or the school lunchbox. Please use unsulphured dried fruits.

Makes one 20cm/8in cake

GF WF DF NF V **OPTIONAL** EF YF

130g/scant 1 cup pitted dates, chopped

200g/1 cup ready-to-eat pitted prunes, chopped

Finely grated zest of 1 unwaxed organic orange

250ml/1 cup unsweetened orange juice

2 heaped tablespoons organic golden (corn) syrup

225g/2 cups gluten-free flour mix

2 teaspoons mixed spice* (pie spice)

2 teaspoons cinnamon

3 teaspoons gluten-free baking powder

350g/2½ cups mixed unsulphured dried fruits

75g/generous ½ cup dried cherries or cranberries

3 tablespoons good Brandy or fresh apple juice if not appropriate or on a yeast-free diet

3 large organic free-range egg whites, stiffly beaten or 3 heaped teaspoons Orgran No Egg egg replacer and 6 tablespoons cold filtered water

Toppings (choose according to taste and diet)

Christmas topping A: 2 tablespoons smooth apricot jam (jelly), warmed through until melted

425g/15oz mixed glacé whole fruits and a festive ribbon to tie around cake

Christmas topping B: 2 tablespoons of smooth apricot jam (jelly)

310g/11oz of your favourite ready-made icing* (confectioners icing) (Super Cook brand Royalice is quick and gluten-free)

Christmas decorations and ribbon

Family tea or lunch box: Sieved icing (confectioners) sugar mixed with a little cold filtered water and a few drops of either Boyajian pure lemon or orange oil (see stockist page 197) – just enough to drizzle all over the cake and down the sides but firm enough to set

20.5cm/8in round, loose-bottomed non-stick cake tin, lightly greased and lined with baking parchment (wax paper)

coeliacs please use gluten-free ingredients

Preheat the oven to 180°C/350°F/Gas mark 4.

Combine the dates, prunes and orange zest in a saucepan. Pour in the orange juice and bring to the boil. Reduce the heat and simmer at bubbling point for 10 minutes or until the fruit is soft. Stir in the syrup and then leave the mixture to cool. Once the mixture has cooled, place it in a food processor, beat to a purée then leave to cool completely.

Meanwhile, sift the flour, spices, baking powder and egg replacer, if using, into a big bowl. Stir in all the mixed dried fruits and dried cherries with the brandy or apple juice and the 6 tablespoons of water to make up the egg replacer, if using. If you are using egg whites, simply fold the stiffly beaten egg whites into the date, flour and fruit mixture with a metal spoon.

Scrape the date mixture out of the food processor and stir into the cake mixture, folding and blending in all the flour and fruit. Transfer the cake mixture to the prepared tin, gently level the surface and cover the top of the tin loosely with foil or baking parchment (wax paper). Bake for 45 minutes, then remove the covering and bake for 30 minutes more or until a skewer, inserted in the cake, comes out clean. Remove the cake from the oven and when it is cold, take it out of the tin and peel off the lining paper.

Christmas topping A: Brush the cake with the melted jam (jelly) and decorate the top of the cake with ever decreasing circles of your favourite glacé fruits (some fruits may need to be halved). Tie a ribbon around the cake and serve. Keep stored in an airtight container over Christmas.

Christmas topping B: Brush the melted jam (jelly) all over the top and sides of the cake. Roll out the icing and cover neatly, sealing the edges and then decorate.

For the family or lunchbox cake, simply mix the icing sugar in a little bowl with a very little water and the flavoured oil until it is just runny enough to drizzle all over the top of the cake. It will keep well in an airtight container for about a week.

Another option – if nuts and eggs can be tolerated – is to go for a nutty and eggy topping. Melt 2 tablespoon of your favourite jam (jelly) and brush it over the top and sides of the cake. Roll out 455g/1lb gluten-free ready-made marzipan (Supercook is good) according to the instructions on the packet, cover the cake with it and tuck and trim until you have a smooth covering. Make up your favourite gluten-free icing, cover the cake and decorate. Keep stored in an airtight container over Christmas.

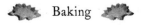 Baking

Easter Chocolate Nest

Yippee! More chocolate! Kids love baking with chocolate and I was no exception, spending afternoons with my grandmother making sponges and puddings. What I treasure most is that baking in her snug little kitchen was taught with love and afterwards the whole family ate the cake together for tea. I wish more children nowadays could share this joy.

Makes one 22cm/8in ring cake

Chocolate cake
150g/5½ × 1oz squares dairy- and nut-free dark chocolate*, broken up
85g/3oz soft dairy-free margarine
100g/scant ½ cup unrefined caster (superfine) sugar
4 large organic free-range eggs, separated and at room temperature
2 heaped tablespoons organic dairy-free cocoa powder*, sieved
60g/½ cup gluten-free flour mix, sieved

Icing
85g/3 × 1oz squares dairy- and nut-free dark chocolate*, chopped
60ml/¼ cup hot filtered water
85g/3oz very soft dairy-free margarine
255g/2 cups icing (confectioners) sugar, sieved
1 teaspoon pure vanilla extract
2 heaped tablespoons organic dairy-free cocoa powder* mixed with 60ml/¼ cup boiling filtered water

To decorate
15g/½oz square dairy- and nut-free dark chocolate*
4 × 50g/2oz packets of Whizzers mini speckled chocolate eggs or D&D chocolates foil-covered mini chocolate eggs (see page 194 for both stockists) or other nut- and dairy-free brands*

22 × 6cm/8½ × 2½in ring mould, greased with dairy-free margarine and dusted with gluten-free flour

* coeliacs please use gluten-free ingredients

Preheat the oven to 180°C/350°F/Gas mark 4.

Start by making the chocolate cake. Melt the chocolate and margarine together in a heatproof bowl set over simmering water, stirring from time to time. Meanwhile, in another mixing bowl, whisk together the sugar and egg yolks until thick and creamy. Whisk in the melted chocolate and margarine. Whisk in the cocoa and then gently fold in the flour.

In another bowl, beat the egg whites with a clean whisk until they hold stiff peaks. Mix 1 tablespoon of the egg whites into the chocolate mixture to loosen it and then, a bit more gently, mix in a second tablespoon. Now lightly fold in the remainder of the egg whites using a metal spoon.

Pour and scrape the mixture into the prepared ring mould and place it on the middle shelf of the preheated oven. Bake for about 40 minutes – the cake should still be moist in the centre. Remove from the oven and leave to cool, then, using a small spatula, ease the edge of the cake away from the tin. Repeat this on the inner edge and then carefully turn out the cake on to the plate you wish to serve it on.

When the cake is cool, prepare the icing. First melt the chocolate and water together in a bowl as described above. Stir the chocolate until glossy. Beat the margarine with the icing (confectioners) sugar in a small bowl until combined. Now gradually incorporate the melted cooled chocolate and then stir in the vanilla extract. Beat in the cooled cocoa and water mixture until the icing is smooth.

Once the cake is cold, ice it using a clockwise motion, starting from the top and moving down the outside. Ice the inside of the ring until the cake is completely covered. I prefer it to have a rough finish for a more realistic 'nest' look. Grate the remaining chocolate over the cake. Fill the centre with the speckled eggs or foil covered eggs and serve or cover and chill until needed.

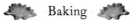

Chocolate Football Birthday Cake

Karen Sullivan, who wrote the introduction to this book and knows an awful lot about kids and food, kindly donated this recipe for me to adapt. Karen has two growing boys, Cole and Luke, to feed and they just love this cake – even if it has got courgettes (zucchini) in it.

If you want to make a make a bigger party cake for 15 older children, double all the quantities and bake in 2 x 23cm/9in tins.

OPTIONAL

Makes about 8 portions

GF · WF · DF · NF · YF · V · EF

---

3 organic-free range eggs or 3 heaped teaspoons Orgran No Egg egg replacer and 6 tablespoons cold water

200g/1 packed cup unrefined soft brown sugar

200g/2 packed cups finely shredded unpeeled organic courgettes (zucchini)

250ml/1 cup unsweetened organic soya plain yogurt or Tofutti Sour Supreme sour cream substitute

125ml/½ cup light sunflower oil

1 teaspoon finely grated unwaxed organic orange rind

1 teaspoon pure vanilla extract

200g/scant 2 cups gluten-free flour mix

30g/⅓ cup dairy-free unsweetened cocoa powder*

2 teaspoons gluten-free baking powder

1 teaspoon gluten-free bicarbonate of soda (baking soda)

1 teaspoon ground cinnamon

Icing

200g/7oz dairy-free margarine

250g/2 cups icing (confectioners) sugar

100g/1 cup dairy-free unsweetened cocoa powder*

Decoration

1½ packets of Whizzers chocolate footballs (available at some superstores and health shops or see page 194 for stockists) or other nut-free brands

2 x 20cm/8in cake tins, each lined with a circle of non-stick baking parchment (wax paper) or 1 x 23cm/9in loose-bottomed, deep, side-release cake tin

* coeliacs please use gluten-free ingredients

Preheat the oven to 180°C/350°F/Gas mark 4.

Beat the eggs and sugar together in a large mixing bowl. Mix in the courgettes (zucchini), yogurt, oil, orange rind and vanilla. In a big bowl, sift together the flour, cocoa, baking powder, bicarbonate of soda (baking soda) and cinnamon and blend into the courgette (zucchini) mixture. If not using eggs, beat the egg replacer, sugar, courgettes (zucchini), yogurt, oil, orange rind and vanilla together with the 6 tablespoons of water.

Pour the batter into the prepared cake tin/s. Bake in the oven until the cakes are just cooked through, about 25 minutes for the 20cm/8in cakes and 45 minutes for the 23cm/9in ones. Remove the cakes from the oven and leave to cool in their tins.

Make the icing when the cake is cold. In a bowl, beat the margarine and icing (confectioners) sugar until light and fluffy using a wooden spoon. Then, using an electric beater, beat in the cocoa until smooth.

Release the cake/s from their tin/s, remove the parchment (wax paper) and place a sponge on a serving plate. Spread a generous amount of the icing mixture over the surface and sides of the cake. If you have made the two smaller cakes, cover the iced cake with the remaining cake and spread the icing all over the cake. Decorate with a ring of footballs. (If you make the single 23cm/9in one larger cake, you will have a bit of spare icing that you can use to decorate some fairy cakes).

Chill the cake in the refrigerator for a few hours or up to 24 hours and serve chilled.

Store any leftovers in an airtight container in the refrigerator.

You can decorate this cake with Whizzers chocolate speckled eggs for Easter or with Whizzers chocolate beans for non-football orientated children or use other gluten-, dairy- and nut-free brands.

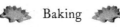 Baking

Apple and Raisin Loaf

As it is made in a loaf tin, this cake is easy to slice and wrap up for a lunchbox or tea. In season, you could also make the cake with ripe pears, which would be just as delicious and, for variety, you could swap the raisins for dried cranberries.

Makes 1 medium loaf

GF   WF   DF   EF   NF   YF   V

100g/3½oz dairy-free margarine, softened

200ml/¾ cup organic runny honey

1½ tablespoons water mixed with 1½ tablespoons cold pressed sunflower oil and 1 heaped teaspoon gluten-free baking powder

1 teaspoon pure vanilla extract

165g/1 cup organic unsulphured raisins

225g/2 cups gluten-free flour mix plus an extra tablespoon to coat the raisins

2 teaspoons arrowroot powder

1 teaspoon gluten-free bicarbonate of soda (baking soda)

2 teaspoons ground cinnamon

A pinch of fine salt (optional)

½ teaspoon freshly grated nutmeg

250ml/1 generous cup unsweetened applesauce made with peeled and cored organic cooking apples and filtered water

1 medium-sized non-stick loaf tin, greased with a little dairy-free margarine

---

Preheat the oven to 180°C/350°F/Gas mark 4.

In a large bowl (or use a food processor), beat the margarine with the honey until light and fluffy. Add the water, oil and baking powder mixture and the vanilla and mix briefly.

Coat the raisins with the tablespoon of flour, which will keep them from sticking together, and set aside.

In a medium-sized bowl, stir together the flour and the remaining dry ingredients. Fold the dry ingredients into the margarine and honey mixture, alternating with the applesauce or, if using the food processor, just blend in the applesauce briefly, then quickly whizz in the dry ingredients. Briefly mix in the raisins and pour the cake mixture into the prepared loaf tin.

Bake the loaf for about 35 minutes until springy to touch on top. You can check that it is cooked through by inserting a skewer into the centre of the loaf, which should come out clean. Cool the loaf in the tin and then turn out to cool completely before serving. Wrap it in foil and store in an airtight container until needed.

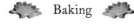 Baking

Chocolate Soda Bread

This great teatime treat is also ideal as a lunchbox treat if it is wrapped in foil. It must be eaten on the day of baking and doesn't need any butter or other spreads with it.

Serves 6–8

450g/4 cups gluten-free white flour mix
2 teaspoons unrefined caster (superfine) sugar
1 teaspoon fine salt
2 teaspoons gluten-free bicarbonate of soda (baking soda)
100g/3½ × 1oz squares dairy- and nut-free chocolate*, roughly chopped
About 400ml/1½–1¾ cups buttermilk

* coeliacs please use gluten-free ingredients

Preheat the oven to 200°C/400°F/Gas mark 6.

Sieve the flour, sugar, salt and bicarbonate of soda (baking soda) into a bowl, mix together and then stir in the chocolate.

Make a well in the centre of the mixture and pour in the buttermilk. Using clean hands, bring the mixture together into a soft but not wet and sticky dough – add a little extra buttermilk if necessary to hold it together. Transfer the dough to a clean board dusted with some gluten-free flour. Knead lightly for a few seconds to tidy it up.

Place the dough on a non-stick baking tray and pat into a thick round about 5cm/2in deep. Using a sharp knife, score deep markings for 6–8 portions and bake in the oven for about 25 minutes until the bread is cooked through.

Serve the bread when it is still just warm but not hot or it will be sticky.

Rye and Oat Soda Bread

This recipe is for those with a wheat allergy or intolerance – it is not suitable for coeliacs. The great thing about soda bread is that not only is it yeast-free but the lack of yeast means there is no rising time and hence it is gloriously quick to make. This loaf is enough to feed a whole troop of children for tea.

Makes one 455g/1lb loaf

170g/1¼ cups organic rye flour
270g/2 scant cups organic oat flour (fine oatmeal)
1 heaped tablespoon organic flax seeds
1 heaped teaspoon gluten-free bicarbonate of soda (baking soda)
A pinch of sea salt
30g/1oz dairy-free margarine
1 heaped teaspoon organic blackstrap molasses
500–600ml/2–2½ cups buttermilk (depending on absorbency of flour)

455g/1lb non-stick loaf tin or a round one if you prefer, greased and floured

Preheat the oven to 220°C/425°F/Gas mark 7.

In a large bowl, mix all the dry ingredients together with your hands, then lightly rub in the margarine and molasses. Make a well in the centre and add the buttermilk. Working with a metal spoon, from the centre, gather the mixture together to make a soft, wet dough. The amount of buttermilk that you use will depend on the absorbency of the flour but the mixture should be 'sticky wet'.

Spoon the dough into the prepared tin and bake for about 35 minutes. Cover the top with foil after 15 minutes. Turn out on to a wire rack and cover with a tea towel. Leave to cool before attempting to cut it.

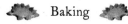

Bacon Cheesy Corn Muffins

If you can't eat bacon and eggs for breakfast, here is an eggless alternative – it is so delicious that everyone will want one.

Makes 8

115g/4oz smoked rindless organic streaky bacon
½ tablespoon cold pressed sunflower oil
55g/2oz dairy-free margarine
300g/2½ cups gluten-free flour mix
3 teaspoons gluten-free baking powder
30g/¼ cup instant polenta or cornmeal
1 teaspoon unrefined caster (superfine) sugar
A pinch of fine salt (optional)
155g/5½oz packet dairy-free grated Cheddar-style hard cheese (see brands and stockists page 192), or a
     yeast-free brand or use goat's or sheep's cheese if not on a dairy-free diet
1 heaped teaspoon Orgran egg replacer and 2 tablespoons of cold filtered water (use 1 organic free-range
     egg if not on an egg-free diet)
300ml/scant 1¼ cups organic unsweetened soya milk (or use rice, oat or almond milk depending on diet)

12-cup, deep muffin tin lined with 8 non-stick paper cases

Preheat the oven to 200°C/400°F/Gas mark 6.

Cook the bacon in the oil in a non-stick frying pan (skillet) for 3–4 minutes until golden. Drain on absorbent kitchen paper, chop the bacon finely and keep to one side. Add the margarine to the pan, remove the pan from the heat and set it aside to allow the margarine to melt slowly.

Sift the flour and baking powder into a large bowl and stir in the polenta or cornmeal, sugar, salt, if using, cooked bacon and three quarters of the cheese. Crack the egg, if using, into a separate bowl and whisk in the milk and melted margarine. If using egg replacer, place it in a bowl with the measured water, then whisk in the milk and melted margarine.

Quickly stir the liquid into the dry ingredients, taking care not to over mix. Divide the mixture between the paper cases, scatter over the reserved cheese and bake for 30 minutes or until well risen and just firm. Transfer to a wire rack and allow to cool slightly.

  Allergy-Free Cooking for Kids

Pick and Mix Muesli

Kids love to do their own thing and giving them the chance to be creative can often mean that you can get them to eat things that they may normally reject on the grounds that they are boring and too healthy to be nice. At the weekend, when all the family are together, arrange a line of bowls filled with groups of the following ingredients on the breakfast table or breakfast bar. They can then pick and mix a super healthy breakfast for themselves.

Choose appropriate sized bowls for the age group:

A bowl of combined organic whole rolled oats* and barley flakes* (coeliacs use organic rice and soy flakes)

A bowl of combined organic buckwheat and millet flakes

A bowl each of unsweetened organic rice krispies and cornflakes (check label for yeast)

80g/¾ cup dried cranberries for the nut-free version *or* for the over fives only and if not on a nut-free diet
   200g/1½ cups whole shelled organic Brazil nuts, roughly chopped

A little bowl or ramekin of organic sesame seeds and organic sunflower seeds

A little bowl of organic pumpkin seeds and organic raisins

A bowl of ready-to-eat dried unsulphured peaches or other dried fruit, roughly chopped

A pinch of ground cinnamon

Chilled organic unsweetened soya milk, rice milk, almond milk or oat milk depending on diet

* coeliacs please use gluten-free ingredients

Choose bowls big enough to suit the number of kids and adults eating breakfast. If you are a single parent with one child then I suggest combining all the flakes in one ramekin, keep the rice krispies and cornflakes separate but combine all the seeds in one ramekin and combine the cranberries or nuts with the raisins. That way you reduce the washing up.

Mix a pinch of cinnamon with the oat and barley mixture if you are using them. Put the chilled milk in a jug and then put all the other ingredients into the chosen bowls. Kids so love pick and mix that with any luck they will pile it high and enjoy it!

Tip all the leftovers into an airtight container and store in a cool place. You can then enjoy eating the muesli yourself for breakfast until you have another pick and mix day.

White Bread

This is the Wellfoods recipe for use in bread makers. It is extremely good and can be sliced and frozen for use in all the usual recipes, such as bread and butter pudding, rusks, stuffings and crumbs for fishcakes or nuggets. I have not used any other brand of flour in this recipe so do use Wellfoods flour.

Makes 1 large loaf

GF WF DF NF V

1 large organic free-range egg

About 600ml/2½ cups filtered water at room temperature

600g/5½ cups Wellfoods gluten-free flour mix (see page 192 for information)

2 teaspoons sea salt

2 tablespoons unrefined granulated sugar

2 tablespoons Trex or other white vegetable fat, at room temperature

2 × 6g–7g/¼oz packs gluten-free, easy-bake style yeast

30g/1oz melted dairy-free margarine

Beat the egg in a measuring jug and add the water to make up 600ml/2½ cups in total. Take the bread maker pan out of the machine, place the liquid mixture into the bread maker pan and add the flour. Put the salt, sugar and vegetable fat into four corners of the pan. Add the yeast in the centre. Replace the pan back in the bread-making machine.

Select the standard bake (wheat) programme appropriate to the machine, extra large loaf and dark crust option. Twenty minutes before the end of baking, carefully lift the lid up and quickly brush the top of the bread with the melted margarine. Close the lid and leave until finished.

Once the baking is completed, carefully lift out the hot pan and turn the hot bread out onto a wire rack to cool. Do not slice until completely cold otherwise the texture will not be quite right. Wrap any leftover bread in clingfilm (plastic wrap) and store in an airtight container for a few days or up to a week. It will need to be toasted after the second day.

Breadsticks

These breadsticks are great for babies to hold and suck or bite. They are also ideal for children to nibble on at parties or on picnics. You can add mixed herbs or finely grated cheese (if not on a dairy-free diet) for older kids. They are so easy to make that you will probably make them regularly rather than just for parties.

Makes 18–24

385g/3½ cups gluten-free white flour mix
14g/2 sachets dried yeast*
4 tablespoons cold pressed extra virgin olive oil and extra for greasing and brushing
250ml/1 cup warm filtered water (amount may vary according to flour absorbency)
Optional – herbs or grated cheese according to age group and allergies

*** coeliacs please use gluten-free ingredients**

Preheat the oven to 180°C/350°F/Gas mark 4.

Put the flour into a large bowl and stir in the yeast. Make a well in the middle and add the oil, the water and any flavouring you may be using. Stir well and bring the dough together into a ball. Knead for about 3 minutes to make a smooth and pliable dough.

Transfer the dough to a clean bowl, cover with a damp cloth and leave in a warm place for about an hour. The dough should have increased in size slightly.

Knead the dough again for a couple of minutes and then divide into 16 small pieces. Roll them into 15cm/6in sticks with warm clean hands, place them well apart on oiled baking trays and brush the sticks with the extra oil. Bake them for about 15–20 minutes until golden. Remove them from the oven and let the breadsticks cool before sticky fingers make a grab for them!

 Baking

Useful information and addresses

Antoinette Savill has a range of delicious, freshly-baked, gluten-, wheat- and dairy-free foods. 'The Antoinette Savill Signature Series' is available from Waitrose, Budgens, The Co-op and other stores and health food shops throughout the UK. The range is also available by mail order from Wellfoods Ltd. The details are listed on page 192.

Vanilla Pod

A new allergy-free Cookery Club for kids

Antoinette Savill and Suki Addington are launching allergy-free cookery classes to teach children between the ages of 5–11 years how to cook seasonal, healthy and fun food.

Suki is a teacher and professional cook and will be organizing the classes in her kitchen in Somerset. The classes will begin in Summer 2003 and be held at the beginning of each school holiday period throughout the year.

For more information, please email www.wheatwatchers.com or telephone Suki Addington on 07711 255409.

Organizations

Institute for Optimum Nutrition
Blades Court
Deodar Road
London SW15 2NU
Telephone: 020 8877 9993

The Coeliac Society
PO Box 220
High Wycombe
Buckinghamshire HP 11 2HY
Telephone: 01494 437278

The Vegetarian Society
Parkdale Dunham Road
Altrincham
Cheshire WA14 4QG
Telephone: 01619 280793

Berrydales Publishers
Berrydale House
5 Lawn Road
London NW3 2XS
Telephone: 020 7722 2866
(Publishers of *The Inside Story* food & health magazine)

British Allergy Foundation
30 Bellegrove Road
Welling
Kent DA16 3PY
Telephone: 020 8303 8525

Stockists

Here is a list of my favourite stockists. I have spent years researching the best and most suitable ingredients for allergy-free recipes and I hope this will be as invaluable to you as it has been for me.

Wellfoods Ltd (Antoinette Savill food range)
Nationwide delivery of gluten- and wheat-free flour, white loaves, bread rolls and pizza bases, which can all be frozen. The bread should be sliced and then frozen in one pack or individually. The rolls should be baked until soft and hot and the pizza can be frozen in quarters or whole. They also have a selection of delicious cakes.

Unit 6 Mapplewell Business Park
Mapplewell
Barnsley S75 6BP
Telephone: 01226 381712
Fax: 01226 381858
Website: www.bake-it.com
Email: wellfoods@bake-it.com

Tofutti UK Ltd (cheeses)
The best range of cream-style cheese dips that I've tasted, in three different flavours. I use it in these recipes – for dips and the cheesecake. The Sour Supreme sour cream substitute is brilliant for potato and pasta salads and puddings. Absolutely delicious frozen range of ice creams that can be used to fill Pavlovas or roulades or served with sauce or fruits. All products, according to Tofutti Ltd, are yeast free, GMO free, lactose free, vegetarian, vegan and kosher.

5th floor
Congress House
14 Lyon Road
Harrow HA1 2FD
Telephone: 020 8861 4443
Fax: 020 8861 0444
Website: www.tofutti.co.uk

The Redwood Wholefood Company (cheeses)

Suppliers of dairy- and lactose-free Cheezly cheeses such as feta-style in oil (brilliant for pizzas, pasta, risotto and salads) and the grated Cheddar-style Cheezly hard cheese, the best alternative that I have found (you'll find I've used it in lots of the recipes). You can buy the cheeses at the on-line shop or at any good health shop.

Redwood House
Burkitt Road
Earlstrees Industrial Estate
Corby
Northamptonshire NN17 4DT
Telephone: 01536 400 557
Fax: 01536 408 878
Website: www.redwoodfoods.co.uk
Email: info@redwoodfoods.co.uk

Orgran Community Foods Ltd (pasta, crumbs and egg replacer)

Stockists of the gluten, wheat-free and yeast-free products, including the pasta that I use in all the recipes, especially the alphabet pasta and the organic rice and corn pasta and lasagne. They also stock breadcrumbs, as well as cookies that can be used for making cheesecake shells. Most important of all is their 'No Egg' natural egg replacer, which I used in most of the recipes – it is gluten, wheat, dairy and yeast free.

Micross
Brent Terrace
London NW2 1LT
Telephone: 020 8208 2966
Fax: 020 8208 1551
Email: sales@communityfoods.co.uk

Allergycare (chocolates)
Suppliers of the brilliant Whizzers dairy-, gluten-, yeast- and wheat-free speckled eggs, chocolate beans, chocolate footballs and other sweeties. Also gluten- and yeast-free baking powder and egg replacer.

Lifestyle Healthcare ltd
Centenary Business Park
Henley-on-Thames
Oxon RG9 1DS
Telephone: 01491 570000
Website: www.gfdiet.com

D & D Chocolates (carob and chocolate)
A very good range of mail order gluten-, wheat-, yeast-, dairy-, sugar-free Christmas chocolates and carob, such as Father Christmas and snowmen. Also Easter eggs and mini eggs, plus goodies such as pralines, couverture bars and peppermint creams. Allergy-free carob flakes and chocolate drops (chips) are also available. They are ideal for decorating cakes, making recipes or as lovely gifts.

261 Forest Road
Loughborough
Leicestershire LE11 3HT
Telephone 01509 216400
Fax: 01509 233961
Website: www.d-dchocolates.com

www.allergyfreedirect.co.uk (dairy-free parmesan & malted rice syrup)
This is a brilliant site for ordering most things that you will need on any of the usual diets. Carob spread, egg replacer, flours, grains and pulses, cereals and baking ingredients. The 24-hour courier service is expensive so its best to go through the site and order anything you may need over the next few months. They also sell gluten-, wheat- and dairy-free cookbooks.

Oxford Wholefoods
5 Centremead
Osney Mead
Oxford OX2 OES
Telephone: 01865 722 003
Fax: 01865 244 134
Email: orders@allergyfreedirect.co.uk

Grano Vita UK Ltd (mayonnaise)

This company make a good organic virgin cold pressed flax oil, which is a rich and natural source of omega-3 oils; a very good egg-free mayonnaise called Mayola which, like all mayonnaise made with vinegar, is not yeast free; and soya milks, which are yeast free.

5 Stanton Close
Finedon Road Industrial estate
Wellingborough
Northamptonshire NN8 4HN
Telephone: 01933 273717

Doves Farm Foods

Nationwide delivery of wheat-free and gluten-free flours and related products

Salisbury Road
Hungerford
Berkshire RG17 0RF
Telephone: 01488 684 880
Website: www.dovesfarm.co.uk

Simply Organic Food Company

Stockists of everything organic – fruit, vegetables, fish, poultry, meat, as well as groceries, baby food, wines and wheat- or lactose-free products. All are delivered to your home or office throughout the UK. Open 24 hours a day, seven days a week.

Freepost, Units Ab2-A6
New Covent Garden Market
London SW8 5YY
Telephone: 0845 1000 444
Fax: 020 7622 4447
Website: www.simplyorganic.net
Email: orders@simplyorganic.net

Broadland Foods

Suppliers of vegetarian and gluten- and wheat-free suet for making sponge puddings and mincemeat.

Great Barr Street
Birmingham B9 4BB
Telephone: 0121 7735955

Sel de Guerande

This sea salt is hand-harvested in the Guerande salt marshes, dried by the sun and wind so that it retains all the magnesium, salts and trace elements.

Telephone: 02 40 62 01 25
Fax: 02 40 62 03 93
Email: isg@seldeguerande.com

Musk's

Makers of sausages since 1884, they now supply gluten-free sausages of various sizes. They have a mail order service with overnight courier, ideal for Christmas hampers and parties all year round.

4 Goodwin Business Park
Newmarket
Suffolk CB8 7SQ
Telephone: 01638 662626
Email: office@musks.com

Paxton & Whitfield

Wonderful mail order goat and sheep cheeses, mild enough for children and perfect for cooking and freezing. They also have a shop in Bath and Stratford upon Avon

93 Jermyn Street
London SW1 Y 6JE
Telephone: 020 7930 0259
Email: sales@cheesemongers.co.uk

The Hive Honey Shop

British honey producers sell their pure honeys here. Mr Hamill, a beekeeper with 150 of his own hives, produces fragrant honeys such as hawthorn, lime, chestnut, heather and wildflower. Mail order is available on their website.

93 Northcote Road
London SW11 6PL
Telephone: 020 7924 6233
Website: www.thehivehoneyshop.co.uk

 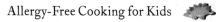

Lakeland Plastics Ltd

Lots of cooking gadgets, including ice cream makers and bread makers. They also sell the Boyajian Pure Citrus oils that I use for flavouring icing and cakes. They are made from cold pressed oils and are very intense – each one takes around 220– 350 limes, lemons or oranges to produce the flavour. Use very little at a time.

Alexandra Buildings
Windermere
Cumbria LA23 1BQ
Telephone: 015394 88100
Website: www.lakelandlimited.co.uk

Index

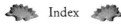 Index